300 Quick Sauces

© Honos Verlag GmbH, a subsidiary of
VEMAG Verlags- und Medien Aktiengesellschaft, Cologne
www.apollo-intermedia.de

Complete production: Honos Verlag GmbH, Cologne
Printed in China

ISBN 3–8299–0839–3

300 Quick Sauces

HONOS VERLAG

Contents

Introduction

The secret to a good sauce lies in its ingredients. They are the alpha and omega of the sauce's aroma and flavour, which in the end make a good meal something special. Here you will discover how to prepare superb sauces.

Introduction

The Sauce: the alpha and omega of every meal

No one knows precisely when the first sauce for a cooked dish was served, but even traditional peoples did not eat their grilled or roasted meat plain, but added seasonings. In time they discovered which seasonings tasted best with which meats, fishes or sorts of vegetables. Eventually they added water or oil, and over time this artistry was increasingly cultivated. A sauce is thus, in essence, nothing more than a seasoning mixture in liquid form.

Sauces were also enjoyed and valued in classical times. According to historic tradition there was a "sauce factory" in Pompeii over two thousand years ago whose most popular sauce was *garum*, a mixture of different seasonings and fish. The sauce was adapted for specific sorts of meat and fish.

The history of sauces can be traced through the centuries into modernity. All cooks who held themselves to high standards created fine sauces for various dishes, and a single dish was often accompanied by several sauces. Cookbooks from earlier times demonstrate that this tradition made its way across all of Europe.

Today we are familiar with recipes for sauces that are prepared with the greatest finesse and the most select ingredients. The basis for a good sauce is an aromatic stock cooked from bones, vegetables, various seasonings and water.

A simpler sauce is the classic roux, which gives a sauce a thick texture, but has a relatively uninteresting flavour. The roux was prepared in simpler cuisine as a sauce for vegetables.

The classic hollandaise, béarnaise and béchamel sauces—whisked together out of butter, milk, eggs and seasonings—are well-known. They have become indispensable, and are used as the basis for myriad variations.

In this book we have collected over three hundred sauces that will add variety and pizzazz to your cooking. From flavourful salad dressings to classics and unusual sauces to accompany pasta, vegetables, meat and fish—including some sweet versions for those of you with a sweet tooth—there is a sauce in this collection for everyone.

You will notice that metric amounts are rounded to their non-metric equivalents. This is especially true of very small amounts. To achieve more precise measurements, we recommend using the metric values.

The sauce recipes all serve four, meaning the given quantities yield approximately 100 to 150 ml (3 to 5 fl oz) per portion of salad dressing and 250 to 350 ml (8–9 to 12 fl oz) per portion of other sauces. The caloric and nutritional values are given per portion.

Happy cooking!

Basic light sauce

5 l (9 pt) poultry stock · 200 g (7 oz) each carrots, leek, onions, celeriac · 50 g (2 oz) butter · 6 tbsp flour · 500 ml (17 fl oz) cream · salt · pepper · dash ground nutmeg

1. Warm the stock in a saucepan. Clean, rinse and if necessary, peel the vegetables and add to the stock. Bring to the boil and reduce to about 1 litre (1 quart).

2. Heat the butter in a second pan and make a roux with the flour. Pour in the stock mixture and bring to the boil while stirring.

3. Strain the sauce through a sieve and mix in the cream. Season to taste.

Per portion ca. 708 kcal/2972 kJ
21 g P · 64 g F · 15 g C

Basic tomato sauce

200 g (7 oz) cubed marbled bacon · 200 g (7 oz) each chopped carrots, leeks, onions, celeriac · 600 g (1 lb 5 oz) tomato purée · 500 g (17 oz) cubed and peeled tomatoes · 5 l (9 p) vegetable broth · 2 cloves garlic, chopped · 1/2 bunch thyme, chopped · 50 g (2 oz) butter · 6 tbsp flour · salt · pepper · paprika

1. Render the bacon in a pot and sauté the vegetables in it. Stir in the tomato purée and tomatoes and pour in the vegetable broth.

2. Add the garlic and thyme and reduce to about 1 litre (1 quart). Strain the stock through a sieve.

3. Melt the butter and make a roux with the flour. Add the stock while stirring and simmer 5 minutes. Season to taste.

Per portion ca. 725 kcal/3045 kJ
30 g P · 21 g F · 102 g C

Basic brown sauce

4 kg (8 lb 13 oz) veal bones · 200 g (7 oz) each chopped carrots, leeks, celeriac and onions · 4 cloves garlic, crushed · 200 g (7 oz) tomato purée · 1/2 bunch thyme, chopped · 2 bay leaves · 500 ml (17 fl oz) red wine · 50 g (2 oz) butter · 6 tbsp flour · salt · pepper · paprika

1. Place veal bones, vegetables, garlic and tomato purée in a pot with 4 l (7 pt) water.

2. Add thyme, bay leaves and red wine and reduce the mixture to about 1 litre (1 quart). Strain through a sieve.

3. Melt the butter and make a roux with the flour. Add the stock while stirring and simmer 5 minutes. Season to taste.

Per portion ca. 293 kcal/1229 kJ
6 g P · 11 g F · 21 g C

Basic sauces

Béarnaise sauce

5 tbsp dry white wine · 5 tbsp white wine vinegar · 2 chopped shallots · 4 tbsp chopped tarragon · 10 crushed peppercorns · 4 egg yolks · 250 g (9 oz) chilled butter · salt · white pepper · cayenne pepper

1. Bring the white wine and vinegar to a boil in a pot, add shallots and herbs and reduce by one third.

2. Pour through a sieve into a metal bowl and gently stir in the egg yolks. Warm the bowl over a double boiler and gradually add the butter until the sauce turns creamy. Do not boil!

3. Season the sauce with salt, pepper and cayenne pepper.

Per portion ca. 560 kcal/2352 kJ
5 g P · 60 g F · 3 g C

Béchamel sauce

30 g (1 oz) butter · 30 g (1 oz) flour · 500 ml (17 fl oz) milk · 1 peeled onion · 1 bay leaf · 3 cloves · salt · white pepper · 5 tbsp cream · ground nutmeg

1. Heat the butter. Stir the flour into hot butter to make a roux and cook 2–3 minutes. Add the milk while stirring and bring to the boil.

2. Stud the onion with the cloves and bay leaf and add to the sauce. Season with salt and pepper and simmer about 15 minutes.

3. Remove the onion. Blend in the cream, more salt and pepper, and season with nutmeg.

Per portion ca. 179 kcal/750 kJ
5 g P · 11 g F · 14 g C

Hollandaise sauce

50 ml (2 fl oz) white wine · 1/2 tbsp crushed peppercorns · 4 egg yolks · 200 g (7 oz) clarified butter · salt · lemon juice

1. Heat the white wine and peppercorns with 4 tbsp water in a pot and reduce by about a third. Strain through a sieve into a metal bowl. Let cool.

2. Place the metal bowl over a double boiler of simmering water, add the egg yolks and whisk until foamy. Be careful that they do not cook!

3. Add the clarified butter while stirring until the sauce is creamy and thickened. Season to taste with salt and lemon juice.

Per portion ca. 458 kcal/1922 kJ
4 g P · 49 g F · 1 g C

Red butter sauce

2 tbsp sugar · 2 red onions · 250 ml (9 fl oz) red wine · 1 branch thyme · 200 ml (7 fl oz) port · 100 g (3.5 oz) chilled butter, cubed · salt · pepper

1. Slice the onions. Caramelise the sugar in a pot, then glaze the onions in it. Add the red wine and cook until reduced by half.

2. Add the thyme and port and reduce further to 150 ml (5 fl oz). Strain the sauce through a sieve, return it to the pot and stir in the butter cubes.

3. Season the sauce to taste with salt and pepper.

White butter sauce

2 cubed shallots · 2 tbsp butter · 1 tbsp wine vinegar · 200 ml (7 fl oz) wine · 150 g (5 oz) chilled butter · salt · pepper · 2 tbsp whipped cream

1. Sauté the shallots in hot butter. Pour in the vinegar and wine and reduce by half.

2. Strain the sauce through a sieve, pour it back into the pot and gradually add the chilled butter, cut into cubes.

3. Season the sauce with salt and pepper and fold in the cream.

Mayonnaise

2 egg yolks · salt · 1/2 tsp mustard · 250 ml (9 fl oz) vegetable oil · pepper · 1–2 tsp lemon juice

1. Gently combine the egg yolks, salt and mustard in a bowl and let stand about 1 minute.

2. Drizzle the oil into the yolk mixture and blend with a hand mixer or a whisk. Gradually mix more vigorously, always adding as much oil as the yolk mixture absorbs. Mix until creamy.

3. Season with pepper and lemon juice, adding more salt if necessary.

Per portion ca. 330 kcal/1386 kJ
1 g P · 21 g F · 12 g C

Per portion ca. 365 kcal/1533 kJ
1 g P · 36 g F · 3 g C

Per portion ca. 593 kcal/2489 kJ
2 g P · 66 g F · 1 g C

Salad dressings

Dressings give a salad the right pizzazz.
Whether it's made with oil and vinegar or
a creamy mayonnaise or yoghurt base,
you'll find just the right dressing for every
salad in the following pages.

Salad dressings

Simple salad dressing

Ingredients

1 onion

2–3 tbsp fruit or wine vinegar

3 tbsp sunflower seed oil

salt

pepper

1. Peel and chop the onion finely.

2. Mix the onion with the vinegar and oil and season with salt and pepper to taste.

Good with leafy green salads.

Per portion ca. 86 kcal/362 kJ
1 g P · 9 g F · 1 g C

Variation 1

Mix the salad dressing with 1 crushed clove of garlic, 2 tbsp chopped mixed herbs and 1 tsp Dijon mustard. **Good with tossed salads.**

Per portion ca. 89 kcal/375 kJ
1 g P · 9 g F · 2 g C

Variation 2

Prepare the salad dressing with balsamic vinegar and olive oil. **Good with tomato salad and carpaccio.**

Per portion ca. 86 kcal/363 kJ
1 g P · 9 g F · 2 g C

Variation 3

Prepare the salad dressing with 2 tbsp red wine vinegar, 1 tsp lemon juice and 1 tbsp sherry, adding 1 tbsp chopped dill. **Good with asparagus salad.**

Per portion ca. 90 kcal/379 kJ
1 g P · 9 g F · 2 g C

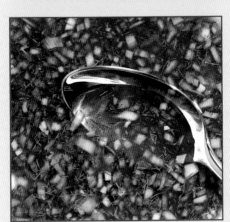

Variation 4

Prepare the salad dressing with 3 tbsp white wine vinegar and 4 tbsp chilli oil and mix in 1–2 tbsp chopped fresh coriander. **Good with vegetable and rice salad.**

Per portion ca. 100 kcal/419 kJ
1 g P · 10 g F · 3 g C

Salad dressings

Herb dressing

100 ml (3 fl oz) safflower oil · 50 ml (2 fl oz) white wine vinegar · 1 tbsp finely chopped parsley · 1 tbsp finely chopped chives · 1 tbsp finely chopped dill · 1 tbsp finely chopped chervil · 1 tbsp finely chopped basil · 1/4 tsp salt · 1/4 tsp pepper · 1 pinch cayenne pepper

Mix the oil, vinegar and herbs together in a bowl. Season with salt, pepper and cayenne pepper and let the dressing marinate for about 12 hours. **For leafy green, vegetable, pasta and rice salads.**

Per portion ca. 229 kcal/964 kJ · 0 g P · 25 g F · 1 g C

Basil dressing

2 cloves garlic · 1 large bunch basil · salt · 1 tbsp white balsamic vinegar · 6 tbsp extra virgin olive oil · 2 tbsp freshly grated parmesan cheese · pepper

Peel the garlic, wash and spin dry the basil. Mince the garlic, basil, a pinch of salt and the balsamic vinegar in a food processor. While the food processor is running, drizzle in the olive oil until it is well blended with the herb-vinegar mixture. Pour into a bowl and stir in the cheese. Season with pepper to taste. **For leafy green and vegetable salads.**

Per portion ca. 174 kcal/733 kJ · 1 g P · 19 g F · 1 g C

Mustard-cream dressing

1/2 tbsp salt · 1/2 tbsp ground mustard seed ·
1 tbsp sugar · 1 egg · 2 tbsp melted butter · 175 g (6 oz)
cream · 1/2 tsp black pepper · 50 ml (2 fl oz) sherry vinegar

Mix together the salt, mustard seed, sugar, egg, butter,
cream and pepper. Add the vinegar while stirring. Over a
double boiler, beat the dressing until it thickens. Let cool.
Good with green salads.

Per portion ca. 72 kcal/303 kJ · 2 g P · 6 g F · 2 g C

Dill dressing

1 bunch dill · 100 ml (3 fl oz) sour cream ·
4 tbsp cream · 2 tbsp lemon juice · salt · pinch cayenne
pepper · Worcestershire sauce

Wash and spin dry the dill, remove stems and chop finely.
Beat the sour cream, cream and lemon juice until foamy
and season with salt, cayenne pepper and Worcestershire
sauce. Stir in the dill. **Good with fish, cucumber and
potato salads.**

Per portion ca. 67 kcal/283 kJ · 1 g P · 6 g F · 3 g C

Salad dressings

Sherry dressing

3 tbsp sherry vinegar · 2 tbsp dry sherry · 1 tsp herb mustard · pinch sugar · 1/4 tsp salt · pinch cayenne pepper · white pepper · 5 tbsp grape seed oil

Stir together the vinegar, sherry, mustard, sugar, salt, cayenne and white pepper until the sugar dissolves. Gradually whisk in the oil until mixture becomes a creamy sauce. **Good with leafy green salads.**

Per portion ca. 45 kcal/189 kJ
0 g P · 4 g F · 1 g C

Yoghurt dressing

150 g (5 oz) plain yoghurt · 3 tbsp sour cream · juice of 1 lemon · 1 tbsp chopped fresh chives · 1 tbsp chopped fresh parsley · salt · white and cayenne pepper · 2 tbsp olive oil

Mix together the yoghurt, sour cream, lemon juice and herbs. Season to taste with salt, white pepper and cayenne pepper. Lastly, gradually blend in the oil. **Good with leafy green salads.**

Per portion ca. 106 kcal/445 kJ
2 g P · 10 g F · 3 g C

Red wine dressing

1 tbsp chopped shallots · 200 ml (7 fl oz) red wine · 4 tbsp red wine vinegar · 1 egg yolk · 1 tsp mustard · 1/2 tsp salt · black pepper · 100 ml (3 fl oz) sunflower oil

Combine shallots, red wine and vinegar in a pan and reduce by half. Let cool. Stir in the egg yolk, mustard and spices, then gradually add oil. Whisk to a creamy sauce. **Good with leafy green and vegetable salads.**

Per portion ca. 280 kcal/1176 kJ
1 g P · 27 g F · 2 g C

Lemon-gruyere dressing

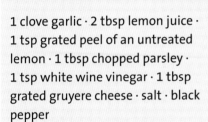

1 clove garlic · 2 tbsp lemon juice ·
1 tsp grated peel of an untreated
lemon · 1 tbsp chopped parsley ·
1 tsp white wine vinegar · 1 tbsp
grated gruyere cheese · salt · black
pepper

Peel and finely chop the garlic, then
combine with the other ingredients,
drizzling olive oil in last until the
dressing has a creamy consistency.
Good with pasta salads.

Per portion ca. 340 kcal/1428 kJ
0 g P · 37 g F · 1,5 g C

Tomato dressing

2 sun-dried tomatoes in oil · 1 clove
garlic · 1 tbsp capers · 6 pitted black
olives · 2 tbsp balsamic vinegar ·
75 ml (2.5 fl oz) extra virgin olive oil ·
1 pinch sugar · black pepper

Chop the tomatoes, peeled garlic,
capers and olives in a food processor.
Add the vinegar and oil, stirring the
mixture into a smooth paste. Season
with sugar and pepper. **Good with
leafy green and vegetable salads.**

Per portion ca. 255 kcal/1071 kJ
1 g P · 27 g F · 3 g C

Yoghurt-orange dressing

100 g (3.5 oz) plain yoghurt · 100 ml
(3 fl oz) whipping cream · juice of
1 orange · salt · black pepper

Stir the yoghurt, cream and orange
juice together in a bowl. Season with
salt and pepper. **Good with leafy
green, rice and pasta salads.**

Per portion ca. 108 kcal/455 kJ
2 g P · 8 g F · 6 g C

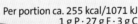

Salad dressings

Peanut dressing

100 g (3.5 oz) peanut butter · 100 ml (3 fl oz) plain yoghurt · 1 tbsp soy sauce · 1 clove garlic · 2 tbsp sesame oil · 2 tbsp white wine vinegar · 3 tbsp chopped flat-leaf parsley

Stir the peanut butter with the yoghurt, soy sauce, peeled and chopped garlic clove, oil and vinegar. Gently blend in the parsley. Allow to marinate thoroughly. **Good with pasta salads.**

Per portion ca. 191 kcal/804 kJ · 8 g P · 16 g F · 4 g C

Thousand island dressing

1 hard-cooked egg · 1/2 onion · 2 tbsp stuffed olives · 1/2 gherkin · 225 ml (8 fl oz) mayonnaise · 2 tbsp chilli sauce or tomato ketchup · 1 tbsp chopped fresh chives · salt · black pepper · 1 tbsp lemon juice

Peel and chop the egg and onion. Finely chop the olives and gherkin. Stir all ingredients together and mix well. This dressing keeps about 1 week in the refrigerator. **Good with egg and vegetable salads in particular, but suitable for all other salad types as well.**

Per portion ca. 465 kcal/1953 kJ · 3 g P · 49 g F · 4 g C

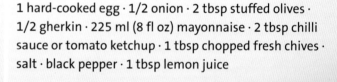

Blue cheese dressing

100 g (3.5 oz) blue cheese (such as Roquefort) · 2 tbsp sour cream · 2 tbsp mayonnaise · 1 tbsp wine vinegar · salt · white pepper · lemon juice

Place the cheese in a bowl and mash with a fork or purée in a food processor. Mix the sour cream, mayonnaise and vinegar with the cheese and season with salt, pepper and lemon juice. Keeps for about 1 week in the refrigerator. **Especially good with iceberg lettuce, Chinese cabbage and white cabbage salads.**

Per portion ca. 138 kcal/581 kJ · 5 g P · 12 g F · 1 g C

Cream cheese-herb dressing

80 g (2.75 oz) cream cheese · 100 ml (3 fl oz) buttermilk · 1 tbsp lemon juice · 2 tsp chopped mixed herbs · salt · black pepper · curry powder

Blend the cream cheese and buttermilk together. Add the lemon juice and herbs, mixing in well. Add savoury flavour with salt, pepper and curry powder to taste. **Good with vegetable salads and poultry.**

Per portion ca. 82 kcal/345 kJ · 3 g P · 6 g F · 2 g C

Salad dressings

Melon juice-wine dressing

50 ml (2 fl oz) melon juice · 1 tbsp honey · 2 tbsp tomato purée · 80 ml (2.5 fl oz) white wine · salt · white pepper · 5 drops Tabasco Sauce · 2 tbsp sunflower oil

Combine the melon juice, honey and tomato purée, then add white wine and season with salt, pepper and Tabasco Sauce. Add the oil last. **Good with leafy green salads with fruit and poultry.**

Per portion ca. 52 kcal/218 kJ
0 g P · 2 g F · 4 g C

Mango dressing

1 ripe mango · juice of 1 lemon · 1 tbsp Dijon mustard · 1/8 tsp chilli powder · 2 tbsp chopped fresh chives · salt · black pepper

Peel the mango, remove the stone and purée the fruit with the lemon juice. Strain the purée through a sieve to remove mango fibres. Mix the mango purée with remaining ingredients. Keeps about a week in the refrigerator. **Good with leafy green salads.**

Per portion ca. 28 kcal/116 kJ
0 g P · 0 g F · 5 g C

Lime-honey dressing

1 lime · 2 tsp mustard with seeds · 1/2 tsp honey · 1/2 bunch fresh basil, chopped · 6 tbsp cold-pressed sunflower seed oil · salt · pepper

Squeeze the lime and mix the juice with the remaining ingredients. Beat vigorously, until the dressing is creamy. **Good with seafood salads.**

Per portion ca. 179 kcal/751 kJ
0 g P · 19 g F · 1 g C

Orange dressing

100 g (3.5 oz) plain yoghurt · 2 tbsp soy sauce · juice of 1/2 orange · 1 tsp tomato purée · 1/2 tsp curry powder · salt · white pepper

Mix the yoghurt with the soy sauce, orange juice and tomato purée, then season with curry powder, salt and pepper. **Good with salads with fruits and vegetables.**

Per portion ca. 26 kcal/109 kJ
1 g P · 1 g F · 2 g C

Pear dressing

4 tbsp pear juice · 1 tsp mustard with seeds · 1/2 clove garlic, crushed · 1 tbsp white wine vinegar · 3 tbsp cold-pressed olive oil · 1 tbsp chopped chives

Blend pear juice with the mustard, garlic and vinegar, then vigorously beat in the olive oil until the sauce is creamy. Stir in the chives. **Good with raw vegetables and leafy green salads.**

Per portion ca. 87 kcal/364 kJ
0 g P · 9 g F · 1 g C

Poppy-sesame dressing

4 tbsp sesame oil · 1 tsp poppy seeds · 2 tbsp apple cider vinegar · 40 g (1.5 oz) roasted cashew nuts, ground · salt · black pepper

Blend the oil and poppy seeds. Add the vinegar and cashews, stirring together until smooth. Season with salt and pepper. **Good with cabbage salads.**

Per portion ca. 107 kcal/449 kJ
2 g P · 9 g F · 3 g C

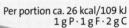

Salad dressings

Vinaigrette

1/2 tsp salt · 1/8 tsp freshly ground pepper · 5 tbsp wine vinegar · 2 tsp Dijon mustard · 175 ml (6 fl oz) olive oil

Whisk all the ingredients together in a bowl. Store dressing in the refrigerator. Keeps about 3 days. **Good with all leafy green salads.**

Per portion ca. 407 kcal/1711 kJ
0 g P · 44 g F · 1 g C

Vinaigrette with pesto

6 tbsp apple cider vinegar · 4 tbsp pesto · 150 ml (5 fl oz) olive oil · salt · black pepper

Combine vinegar and pesto in a bowl. Slowly whisk in the oil until well blended. Season the vinaigrette to taste with salt and pepper, adding more vinegar if necessary. **Good with pasta, vegetable, beef and poultry salads.**

Per portion ca. 335 kcal/1407 kJ
0 g P · 37 g F · 0 g C

Vinaigrette with maple syrup

3 tbsp apple cider vinegar · 3 tbsp maple syrup · 1 tsp Dijon mustard · 8 tsp grape seed oil · salt · pepper

Briefly heat the vinegar and syrup in a saucepan. Blend in mustard and oil, stirring until sauce has a homogeneous consistency. Salt and pepper to taste. Pour the vinaigrette on the salad while warm. **Good with vegetable and rice salads.**

Per portion ca. 103 kcal/435 kJ
0 g P · 10 g F · 3 g C

Beetroot dressing

Red currant dressing

Garlic dressing

40 g (1.5 oz) beetroot (from a jar) ·
125 ml (4 fl oz) vegetable broth ·
1 tsp white wine vinegar · salt ·
white pepper · 1 pinch sugar · 3 tbsp
safflower oil

150 g (5 oz) each sour cream, plain
yoghurt · 50 g (2 oz) curried ketchup ·
1 tbsp currant jelly · 1 pinch paprika ·
1 pinch cayenne · 4 tbsp fruit vinegar
· salt · black pepper

2 garlic cloves · 100 g (3.5 oz)
mayonnaise · 4 tbsp cream · 2 tbsp
sour cream · salt

Purée the beetroot until smooth. Mix
with the broth, vinegar, spices and
sugar. Add the oil last, slowly pour it
into the mixture and blending well.
Good with potato salad.

Mix together the sour cream,
yoghurt, ketchup and currant jelly.
Season with the paprika, cayenne,
vinegar, salt and black pepper. **Good
with pasta and rice salads.**

Peel and crush the garlic cloves. Mix
the garlic with the mayonnaise,
cream and sour cream. Season with
salt to taste. **Good with poultry and
fish salads.**

Per portion ca. 47 kcal/199 kJ
0 g P · 4 g F · 2 g C

Per portion ca. 93 kcal/392 kJ
3 g P · 5 g F · 7 g C

Per portion ca. 219 kcal/920 kJ
1 g P · 24 g F · 1 g C

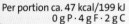

Salad dressings

Horseradish-anchovy dressing

175 g (6 oz) mayonnaise · 1 tbsp horseradish (from a jar) · 1 tsp finely chopped anchovies · 1 tsp grated onion · 1 tsp Worcestershire sauce · 1/4 tsp Tabasco Sauce

Thoroughly blend the mayonnaise, horseradish, anchovies and onion. Season to taste with Worcestershire sauce and Tabasco Sauce. **Good with leafy green, vegetable, and potato salads.**

Per portion ca. 335 kcal/1407 kJ · 1 g P · 36 g F · 2 g C

Tarragon-chervil dressing

2 tbsp finely chopped tarragon · 2 tbsp finely chopped chervil · 200 g (7 oz) crème fraîche · 2 tbsp sherry · 2 tbsp rosé wine · salt · black pepper

Blend the herbs with the crème fraîche, sherry and wine. Season to taste with salt and pepper. Allow the dressing to marinate in the refrigerator for an hour, then adjust seasoning. **Good with mushroom and pasta salads.**

Per portion ca. 151 kcal/635 kJ · 1 g P · 15 g F · 2 g C

Coconut-chilli sauce

3 tbsp grape seed oil · 1–2 finely chopped red chillies · 3 finely chopped shallots · 1 crushed garlic clove · 75 ml (2.5 fl oz) coconut milk (tinned) · juice of 1 lime · salt

Heat the grape seed oil and cook the chillies, shallots and garlic in it until soft. Add the coconut milk to this mixture and heat gently. Season to taste with lime juice and salt. Allow to cool. **Good with vegetable, rice and pasta salads.**

Per portion ca. 59 kcal/250 kJ · 1 g P · 5 g F · 2 g C

Peanut-chilli dressing

5 tbsp peanut oil · 30 g (1 oz) peanuts · 2 tbsp light soy sauce · 3 tbsp white balsamic vinegar · 1 pinch chilli powder · salt · black pepper

Heat the peanut oil. Finely chop the peanuts and roast them in the oil. Add the soy sauce and stir to blend. Allow to cool, then season to taste with the vinegar, chilli powder, salt and black pepper. **Good with leafy green and mushroom salads.**

Per portion ca. 104 kcal/439 kJ · 2 g P · 10 g F · 1 g C

Salad dressings

Apple-orange dressing

1 tsp apple juice concentrate · 2 tbsp balsamic vinegar · 2 tbsp orange juice · salt · black pepper · 4 tbsp olive oil

Blend together the apple juice concentrate with the balsamic vinegar and orange juice. Season to taste with salt and black pepper, then gradually add the olive oil, stirring with a whisk until the sauce has a homogeneous consistency. **Good with leafy and wild green salads.**

Per portion ca. 109 kcal/458 kJ
9 g P · 12 g F · 1 g C

Two-oil dressing

3 tbsp red wine vinegar · salt · black pepper · 3 tbsp hazelnut oil · 3 tbsp olive oil

Stir together the red wine vinegar, salt and black pepper. Slowly add the two types of oil and blend well. **Good with mixed leafy green and fruit salads such as avocado.**

Per portion ca. 115 kcal/483 kJ
10 g P · 13 g F · 1 g C

Sesame dressing

50 ml (2 fl oz) maize oil · 50 ml (2 fl oz) rice wine vinegar· 2 tbsp dark soy sauce · 1 crushed clove garlic · salt · black pepper · 2 tbsp sesame oil

Blend together the maize oil, rice wine vinegar and dark soy sauce with the crushed clove of garlic. Season to taste with salt and black pepper. Finally, whisk in the sesame oil until the dressing is creamy. **Good with meat salads.**

Per portion ca. 141 kcal/592 kJ
1 g P · 15 g F · 1 g C

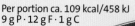

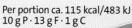

Pumpkin oil vinaigrette

2 tbsp red wine vinegar · 2 tbsp apple cider vinegar · 2 tsp apple juice concentrate · 2 tsp cold-pressed pumpkin oil · 4 tbsp cold-pressed sunflower seed oil · grated lemon peel from an untreated lemon · white pepper

Combine the vinegars, apple juice concentrate and the pumpkin and sunflower seed oils. Add the grated lemon peel and season with pepper. **Good with Chinese cabbage.**

Per portion ca. 128 kcal/537 kJ
0 g P · 13 g F · 1 g C

Peppermint sauce

100 ml (3 fl oz) cream · juice of 1 lemon · 10 fresh peppermint leaves · 2 tbsp ricotta cheese · salt · white pepper

Mix together the cream and lemon juice until foamy. Wash, rinse and finely chop the fresh peppermint leaves. Stir into the cream mixture with the ricotta cheese. Season to taste with salt and pepper. **Good with pasta or iceberg lettuce salads.**

Per portion ca. 88 kcal/369 kJ
2 g P · 8 g F · 2 g C

Walnut-honey dressing

3 tbsp red wine vinegar · 1 tbsp medium-hot mustard · juice of 1/2 orange · 1 tsp honey · 1 bunch finely chopped mixed herbs · 3 tbsp cold-pressed walnut oil · salt · black pepper

Stir together the vinegar, mustard, orange juice, honey and herbs. Gradually add the walnut oil while whisking and season the dressing to taste with salt and pepper. **Good with endive and radicchio salads.**

Per portion ca. 41 kcal/173 kJ
0 g P · 4 g F · 1 g C

Salad dressings

Warm vinaigrette with thyme

4 tbsp balsamic vinegar · 6 tbsp cold-pressed olive oil · 1 tbsp fresh chopped thyme · 1 tbsp fresh chopped rosemary · salt · pepper

Heat the vinegar, oil, thyme and rosemary in a pan and slowly warm while stirring with a whisk. When it is well heated, remove the sauce from the heat and season to taste with salt and pepper. **Good with tomato salad.**

Per portion ca. 162 kcal/681 kJ · 0 g P · 18 g F · 0 g C

Sesame-lime sauce

3 tbsp sesame butter (tahini) · juice and zest of 1–2 un-treated limes · 1 crushed garlic clove · 1 pinch hot paprika · 1 tbsp chopped coriander leaf · salt · black pepper

Mix the tahini with the lime juice and zest, garlic and paprika. Add the coriander leaf and season to taste with salt and pepper. **Good with aubergine salad.**

Per portion ca. 35 kcal/146 kJ · 1 g P · 2 g F · 2 g C

Malt vinegar-rapeseed oil dressing

3 tbsp rapeseed oil · 1 tbsp lemon juice · 1 tbsp tomato
purée · 1 tbsp malt vinegar · 1 tbsp chopped flat leaf
parsley

Stir the rapeseed oil, lemon juice, tomato purée and malt
vinegar into a smooth sauce. Finally stir in the parsley.
Good with legume salads.

Per portion ca. 36 kcal/150 kJ · 0 g P · 4 g F · 0 g C

Walnut-honey sauce

6 tbsp walnut oil · 3 tbsp white balsamic vinegar · 1 tsp
filtered honey · 1 tsp Dijon mustard · 1 pinch ground
ginger · salt · black pepper

Blend together the walnut oil, balsamic vinegar, honey
and mustard until smooth. Season with ginger, salt and
pepper. **Good with leafy green salads with feta cheese.**

Per portion ca. 142 kcal/596 kJ · 0 g P · 15 g F · 2 g C

Salad dressings

Green dressing

50 g (2 oz) mixed herbs · 50 g (2 oz) spinach · 250 g (9 oz) mayonnaise (see p. 11)

Wash and rinse the herbs and spinach and blanch in boiling water for about 30 seconds. Drain, rinse and dry. Chop finely and blend into the mayonnaise. **Good with egg, vegetable, poultry and fish salads.**

Per portion ca. 477 kcal/2005 kJ
2 g P · 52 g F · 3 g C

Caraway seed dressing

115 ml (4 fl oz) sour cream · 115 g (4 oz) mayonnaise (see p. 11) · 5 tbsp white wine vinegar · 1 tsp mustard · 2 tsp ground caraway seeds · 1 pinch sugar · salt · pepper

Blend together thoroughly the sour cream, mayonnaise, vinegar, mustard and caraway seeds. Season with sugar, salt and pepper. **Good with coleslaw and other cabbage salads.**

Per portion ca. 255 kcal/1071 kJ
2 g P · 27 g F · 3 g C

Herb dressing with capers

150 g (5 oz) mayonnaise (see p. 11) · 50 ml (2 fl oz) sour cream · 1 tsp Dijon mustard · 2 tbsp cubed gherkins · 2 tbsp chopped capers · 2 tbsp chopped parsley · 1 tbsp chopped tarragon · salt · pepper

Mix the mayonnaise, sour cream, mustard and other ingredients together. Season to taste with salt and pepper. **Good with cold roasted meat, egg and fish salads and vegetables.**

Per portion ca. 308 kcal/1292 kJ
1 g P · 33 g F · 3 g C

Tomato-chilli dressing

Ginger dressing

Lemon sauce with mint

50 ml (2 fl oz) vegetable broth · 1 tbsp tomato purée · 50 ml (2 fl oz) red wine vinegar · 50 ml (2 fl oz) olive oil · 1/2 tsp chilli powder · 1 tbsp fresh lemon juice · 1 tbsp chopped coriander leaf

Combine all ingredients except for the coriander leaf and blend well. Stir in the coriander at the end. **Good with salads with legumes or pasta salads.**

Per portion ca. 130 kcal/548 kJ
0 g P · 13 g F · 1 g C

1 egg yolk · salt · 1 tsp finely grated ginger · 70 ml (2.5 fl oz) olive oil · 70 ml (2.5 fl oz) walnut oil · 1 tbsp coarsely chopped green onion · black pepper

Blend the egg yolk, salt and ginger in a food processor. With the food processor running, add the olive and walnut oils and blend until smooth. Add the green onions last and mince. Season with black pepper. **Good with poultry, meat and seafood salads.**

Per portion ca. 330 kcal/1386 kJ
1 g P · 37 g F · 1 g C

4 tbsp crème fraîche · grated peel and juice of 1 lemon · 1 tbsp finely chopped mint · 2 tbsp mayonnaise (see p. 11) · 3 tbsp plain yoghurt · salt · black pepper

Mix all the ingredients together thoroughly and season with salt and pepper. **Good with salads made with fresh young vegetables such as snow peas and baby maize.**

Per portion ca. 75 kcal/315 kJ
1 g P · 7 g F · 1 g C

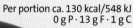

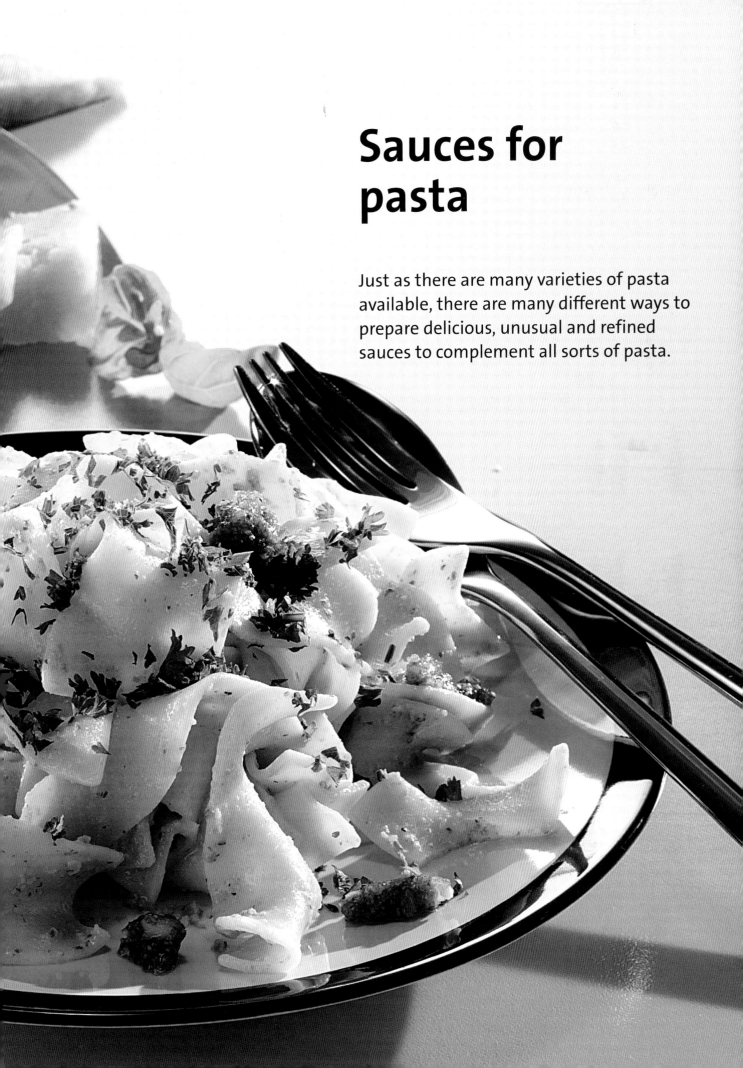

Sauces for pasta

Just as there are many varieties of pasta available, there are many different ways to prepare delicious, unusual and refined sauces to complement all sorts of pasta.

Pasta sauces

Sugo di pomodoro: tomato sauce

800 g (1 lb 12 oz) ripe tomatoes

2 ribs of celery with leaves

1 shallot

20 large basil leaves

2 cloves of garlic crushed with salt

1 bunch fresh parsley, chopped

1 tbsp fresh oregano, chopped

5 tbsp olive oil

black pepper

salt

1. Wash and peel the tomatoes, remove the stems and seeds and chop into cubes. Wash and rinse celery, removing the hard outer fibres. Chop the leaves.

2. Peel the shallot and chop finely. Wash, dry and chop the basil.

3. Keep refrigerated until serving.

Good with all types of pasta.

Per portion ca. 190 kcal/798 kJ
3 g P · 16 g F · 9 g C

Variation 1

Substitute 1 peeled and grated carrot and 100 g (3.5 oz) grated celeriac for the ribs of celery. Render 100 g (3.5 oz) smoked bacon in a pan and blend with the *sugo*. **Good with all types of pasta.**

Per portion ca. 226 kcal/947 kJ
8 g P · 18 g F · 9 g C

Variation 2

Prepare the tomato *sugo* as above, but without olive oil. Heat 1 tbsp butter and 2 tbsp olive oil in a pan and heat the *sugo* in it. Stir in 200 g (7 oz) ricotta cheese. **Good with spaghetti and vermicelli.**

Per portion ca. 177 kcal/743 kJ
8 g P · 13 g F · 7 g C

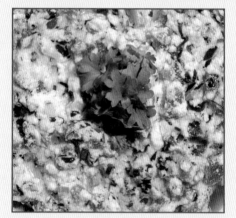

Variation 3

Prepare the tomato *sugo* as above with butter and olive oil. Add 125 ml (4.5 fl oz) white wine and allow to simmer for a short time. Add 100 g (3.5 oz) tunafish or chopped anchovies. **Good with penne and macaroni.**

Per portion ca. 119 kcal/500 kJ
6 g P · 7 g F · 2 g C

Variation 4

Sauté the tomato *sugo* in butter and olive oil. Stir in 1 tbsp capers and 100 ml (3 fl oz) cream and add a touch of chilli oil for aroma. Serve with 50 g (2 oz) grated parmesan cheese. **Good with spaghetti and spaghettini.**

Per portion ca. 255 kcal/1071 kJ
8 g P · 21 g F · 9 g C

Pasta sauces

Pesto Genovese

150 g (5 oz) fresh basil leaves · 2 tbsp pine nuts · 4 cloves garlic · salt · 6 tbsp freshly grated parmesan cheese · 6 tbsp olive oil

Wash and spin-dry the basil. Toast the pine nuts in a pan with no oil. Peel and coarsely chop the garlic, then mince in a food processor. Add the salt, parmesan cheese and olive oil and blend until a creamy sauce forms. **Good with spaghetti, gnocchi, tortellini and ravioli.**

Per portion ca. 273 kcal/1145 kJ · 7 g P · 26 g F · 3 g C

Sauce with garlic and chilli

4 garlic cloves · 1 medium-large red chilli pepper · 100 ml (3 fl oz) olive oil · salt

Peel and chop the garlic finely. Wash, rinse and remove stem from the chilli and chop finely. Heat the olive oil in a pan and sauté the garlic and chilli in it until the oil begins to change colour. Season with salt. Just before serving, add your pasta to the pan and toss it with the sauce. **Good with fettuccine.**

Per portion ca. 224 kcal/941 kJ · 15 g P · 25 g F · 1 g C

Sauce with anchovies and spinach

900 g (2 lbs) spinach · 3 tbsp olive oil · 3 garlic cloves · 60 g (2 oz) anchovies in oil · 1/2 tsp dried chilli flakes

Wash and rinse spinach, then blanch for about two minutes in boiling water. Pour out the water and let drain. Heat the oil in a large pot. Peel and crush garlic, then heat in the oil. Add anchovies and chilli flakes and sauté together while stirring. Add spinach and mix. **Good with linguine and tagliatelle.**

Per portion ca. 142 kcal/600 kJ · 8 g P · 10 g F · 3 g C

Olive and tomato sauce

3 garlic cloves · 30 g (1 oz) sun-dried tomatoes · 2 tbsp olive oil · 375 ml (13 fl oz) vegetable broth · 75 g (2.5 oz) pitted black olives · 2 tbsp chopped fresh basil

Peel and finely chop the garlic. Cut the tomato into small pieces. Heat the oil in a pan and sauté the garlic in it. Add the tomatoes and vegetable broth, bring to the boil and let simmer about 10 minutes over low heat. Chop olives and add to the sauce with the basil. **Good with spaghetti or fettuccine.**

Per portion ca. 140 kcal/588 kJ · 1 g P · 15 g F · 2 g C

Pasta sauces

Herb-cream sauce

1/4 bunch each chopped parsley, chervil, basil, chives · 1 coarsely chopped garlic clove · 50 ml (2 fl oz) white wine · 200 ml (7 fl oz) cream · salt · pepper · nutmeg

Purée the herbs and garlic in a food processor. Heat the white wine in a saucepan, add the cream and season to taste with salt, pepper and nutmeg. Stir in the chopped herbs last. **Good with all types of pasta.**

Per portion ca. 166 kcal/697 kJ
2 g P · 15 g F · 4 g C

Tomato-chervil sauce

2 tbsp olive oil · 300 g (10 oz) peeled and cubed tomatoes · 1 container crème fraîche · salt · pepper · ground nutmeg · 1 tbsp chopped chervil

Heat the oil in a saucepan and braise the tomatoes in it for about 5 minutes. Stir in the crème fraîche and season to taste with the spices. Lastly, add the chervil to the sauce. **Good with fettuccine and spaghetti.**

Per portion ca. 179 kcal/750 kJ
2 g P · 18 g F · 4 g C

Cold capers sauce

50 g (2 oz) capers · 4 anchovies · 50 g (2 oz) pitted black olives · 3 chopped cloves garlic · 8 tbsp olive oil · 3 tbsp lemon juice

Drain the capers and anchovies and chop into small pieces. Chop the olives. Mix all the ingredients except the oil and lemon juice. Slowly beat in the oil and season with lemon juice. **Good with spaghetti, penne and linguine.**

Per portion ca. 330 kcal/1386 kJ
2 g P · 33 g F · 9 g C

Porcini mush-room sauce

30 g (1 oz) dried porcini mushrooms ·
3 tbsp butter · 2 chopped onions ·
250 g (9 oz) sour cream · 3 tbsp
sherry · salt · black pepper

Soften the mushrooms in 750 ml (1
pt 7 fl oz) water. Melt the butter and
sauté the onions in it. Add the mushrooms with their water and the sour
cream. Let simmer for 15 minutes.
Stir in the sherry and season to taste
with salt and pepper. **Good with
spaghetti.**

Per portion ca. 159 kcal/668 kJ
5 g P · 13 g F · 5 g C

Rocket sauce

250 g (9 oz) cream · 150 g (5 oz)
coarsely chopped rocket salad · 175 g
(6 oz) grated pecorino cheese · salt ·
pepper

Heat the cream in a saucepan, then
add the rocket and cheese. Let the
cheese melt while stirring continuously. Season with salt and pepper.
**Good with spaghetti, tagliatelle and
linguine.**

Per portion ca. 253 kcal/1061 kJ
13 g P · 21 g F · 3 g C

Lemon cream sauce

1 untreated lemon · 250 ml (9 fl oz)
cream · 2 tbsp Cognac · juice of
1/2 lemon · salt · white pepper

Grate the peel of the lemon, then
separate the flesh of the lemon and
chop into small cubes. Heat the
cream and cognac, stir in the lemon
cubes and simmer for 5 minutes.
Season to taste with lemon juice, salt
and pepper. **Good with spaghetti,
fettuccine and macaroni.**

Per portion ca. 209 kcal/876 kJ
2 g P · 19 g F · 6 g C

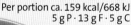
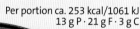

Pasta sauces

Olive sauce

3 tbsp olive oil · 150 g (5 oz) chopped onions ·
1 crushed clove garlic · 2 carrots · 50 g (2 oz) celeriac ·
1 small stem leek · 1 large tin tomatoes (850 g/1 lb 14 oz) ·
salt · pepper · cayenne pepper · sweet paprika powder ·
85 g (3 oz) pitted black olives

Heat the olive oil and sauté the onions and garlic in it.
Wash, peel and cube the carrots, celeriac and leek. Add to
the onions and braise another 5 minutes. Cut the tomatoes
into small pieces and add, along with their juice. Allow the
sauce to cook and thicken. Season with spices. Chop the
olives and stir into sauce. **Good with spaghetti, tagliatelle
and macaroni.**

Per portion ca. 216 kcal/906 kJ · 4 g P · 18 g F · 10 g C

Courgette sauce

500 g (17 oz) courgettes · 200 g (7 oz) cream
cheese · 125 ml (4 fl oz) milk · 100 ml (3 fl oz) dry white
wine · 1 chopped onion · 1 chopped clove garlic · 1 bunch
basil · salt · pepper

Clean and rinse the courgettes, then grate finely. Bring the
cream cheese, milk, wine, onion, garlic and courgettes to
the boil in a pot and simmer 5 minutes. Wash, spin dry
and chop the basil. Stir into the sauce and season to taste
with salt and pepper. **Good with penne, fussili, and
farfalle.**

Per portion ca. 338 kcal/1001 kJ · 9 g P · 17 g F · 7 g C

Asparagus cream sauce

750 g (1 lb 10 oz) green asparagus · 2 tbsp butter ·
1 chopped onion · 250 ml (9 fl oz) cream · 3 peeled and
chopped tomatoes · 250 g (9 oz) sliced cooked turkey
breast · 1/2 bunch each parsley and basil, chopped ·
salt · pepper

Wash and peel the asparagus and cook to al dente in
salted water. Heat the butter in a saucepan and sauté the
onion in it. Add the cream and bring to the boil. Stir in
tomatoes and let simmer 10 minutes. Slice the asparagus
and turkey breast into strips and stir into the sauce with
the herbs. Season with salt and pepper. **Good with
wholegrain noodles.**

Per portion ca. 405 kcal/1701 kJ · 19 g P · 33 g F · 9 g C

Crayfish sauce

200 g (7 oz) freshly shelled peas · 2 courgettes ·
2 carrots · 200 g (7 oz) rocket salad · 2 tbsp butter · 300 g
(10 oz) cooked crayfish · 4 tbsp cream · 2 tbsp sherry · salt ·
pepper · 1/2 bunch dill, chopped

Wash the peas and cook for 5 minutes. Clean, rinse and
dice the courgettes. Peel and grate the carrots. Wash, dry
and chop the rocket. Heat the butter in a pot and sauté
the courgettes and carrots in it for 5 minutes. Add peas,
rocket and crayfish and cook 5 more minutes. Season the
sauce with the remaining ingredients. **Good with
tortellini and ravioli.**

Per portion ca. 214 kcal/899 kJ · 21 g P · 9 g F · 12 g C

Pasta sauces

Parsley sauce with almonds

250 g (9 oz) almonds, coarsely chopped · 3 tbsp parsley · 100 g (3.5 oz) grated Gruyère cheese · 250 ml (9 fl oz) olive oil · 3 tbsp chopped chives · salt · black pepper

Purée the almonds and parsley in a food processor. Add the cheese and blend. Gradually add the oil until a thick paste forms. Season with chives, salt and pepper. **Good with green noodles, spaghetti and gnocchi.**

Per portion ca. 948 kcal/3980 kJ
18 g P · 97 g F · 4 g C

Tomato sauce with butter

100 g (3.5 oz) butter · 5 finely chopped shallots · 700 g (1 lb 8 oz) skinned and chopped tomatoes · salt · black pepper · 3 tbsp chopped fresh basil

Heat the butter in a fry pan and sauté the shallots in it. Add the tomatoes and allow the mixture to cook for about 10 minutes. Season with salt and pepper. Add the basil last. **Good with ravioli and tortellini.**

Per portion ca. 228 kcal/956 kJ
3 g P · 21 g F · 7 g C

Sage sauce with mascarpone

1 handful sage leaves · 2 tbsp butter · 250 ml (9 fl oz) vegetable broth · 150 g (5 oz) mascarpone cheese · 80 g (2.75 oz) freshly grated parmesan cheese

Wash and finely chop the sage leaves. Melt the butter in a saucepan and sauté the sage in it. Pour in the broth. Add both cheeses while continuing to stir. **Good with green and white fettuccine.**

Per portion ca. 246 kcal/1031 kJ
11 g P · 22 g F · 1 g C

Shrimp sauce

200 g (7 oz) butter · 1 finely chopped onion · 1/2 tsp nutmeg · 250 g (9 oz) cooked and peeled shrimp · 3 tbsp freshly chopped dill · salt · black pepper

Melt 50 g (2 oz) of the butter and sauté the onions in it. Add nutmeg and cook briefly. Stir in the rest of the butter and remove pan from the heat. Chop the shrimp finely and mix into the sauce. Season to taste with dill and spices. **Good with tortellini.**

Per portion ca. 443 kcal/1859 kJ
14 g P · 43 g F · 2 g C

Anchovy sauce

50 g (2 oz) anchovies in oil · 1 crushed garlic clove · grated peel of 1 un-treated lemon · 100 g (3.5 oz) butter · black pepper · Worcestershire sauce · 4 tbsp chopped fresh dill

Purée the anchovies with the oil, garlic and lemon peel. Melt the butter and slowly add it to the anchovies. Season to taste with pepper, Worcestershire sauce and the dill. **Good with black noodles.**

Per portion ca. 208 kcal/872 kJ
3 g P · 21 g F · 2 g C

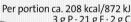

Ricotta sauce

1 tbsp olive oil · 1 finely chopped gar-lic clove · 2 chopped green onions · 8 chopped green olives · 250 g (9 oz) ricotta cheese · 150 g (5 oz) cream cheese · 2 tbsp chopped fresh chervil · salt · black pepper · nutmeg

Heat the oil and sauté the garlic in it for 5 minutes. Let it cool and then combine with the remaining ingre-dients. **Good with pasta salads.**

Per portion ca. 318 kcal/1334 kJ
12 g P · 28 g F · 5 g C

Pasta sauces

Aubergine-honey sauce

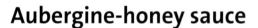

40 g (1.5 oz) butter · 1 aubergine · 2 tbsp liquid honey · 1 tin diced tomatoes (450 g/1 lb) · salt · black pepper · 1/2 bunch each parsley and basil, chopped

Wash and rinse the aubergine, then cut it in cubes. Melt the butter in a saucepan. Stir in the honey and sauté the aubergine in it. Add the tomato and heat through. Season the sauce with salt and pepper, then stir in the chopped herbs. **Good with penne, macaroni, fussili and pappardelle.**

Per portion ca. 117 kcal/493 kJ · 2 g P · 9 g F · 8 g C

Chilli sauce

500 g (17 oz) tomatoes · 1 chilli pepper · 4 tbsp olive oil · 1 chopped onion · 1 chopped clove garlic · 125 ml (4.5 fl oz) vegetable broth · 1 tsp chopped fresh oregano · 2 tbsp chopped parsley · salt · pepper · 15 green olives

Peel, core and dice the tomatoes. Wash the chilli, remove stem and seeds, and chop finely. Heat the oil and sauté the onions and garlic in it. Add the tomatoes and chilli and sauté. Pour the broth onto this mixture and let simmer for 15 minutes. Stir in the herbs and season to taste with salt and pepper. Add sliced olives. **Good with spaghetti, macaroni and farfalle.**

Per portion ca. 242 kcal/1016 kJ · 3 g P · 22 g F · 7 g C

Béarnaise with chives

100 g (3.5 oz) Parma ham · 1 bunch chives ·
350 ml (12 fl) béarnaise sauce (see p. 10) · 2 tbsp sherry ·
salt · white pepper

Slice the ham into fine strips. Wash, spin dry and then
chop the chives. Add the sherry to the béarnaise sauce,
then heat. Stir in the chives and then the Parma ham.
Season with salt and pepper. **Good with green noodles
and fettuccine.**

Per portion ca. 56 kcal/236 kJ · 6 g P · 2 g F · 2 g C

Goat cheese sauce

250 ml (9 fl oz) cream · 100 g (3.5 oz) creamy goat
cheese · 100 g (3.5 oz) Mortadella · 1 bunch fresh chives,
chopped · 2 tbsp chopped walnuts · salt · white pepper

Bring the cream to a boil in a pot and allow to thicken
slightly. Add the goat cheese to the cream while stirring.
Chop the Mortadella into cubes and add it to the sauce.
Stir in the chives and nuts and season with salt and
pepper. **Good with lasagne, gnocchi and ravioli.**

Per portion ca. 353 kcal/1480 kJ · 8 g P · 35 g F · 3 g C

Pasta sauces

Almond-poppy seed sauce

150 g (5 oz) slivered almonds · 65 g (2 oz) butter · 50 g (2 oz) ground poppy seeds · 200 g (7 oz) cream · black pepper

Toast the almonds in a fry pan with no oil, then chop them. Melt the butter in a saucepan, stir in the poppy seeds, sauté briefly, then add the almonds and cream. Add savoury flavour with pepper. **Good with all types of pasta.**

Per portion ca. 540 kcal/2268 kJ
11 g P · 54 g F · 4 g C

Pumpkin sauce

6 tbsp olive oil · 3 finely chopped cloves garlic · 125 ml (4.5 fl oz) white wine · 500 g (17 oz) pumpkin, cooked and puréed · 1/2 bunch each parsley and basil · salt · pepper

Heat the oil and sauté the garlic in it. Pour in the wine and bring to the boil. Stir in puréed pumpkin and simmer 5 minutes. Add the chopped herbs and season with salt and pepper. **Good with fussili.**

Per portion ca. 229 kcal/960 kJ
2 g P · 18 g F · 9 g C

Saffron-leek sauce

100 g (3.5 oz) leek, sliced into rings · 1 tbsp butter · 100 ml (3 fl oz) each white wine, cream, vegetable broth · 1 g saffron · 4 tbsp grated cheese · salt · black pepper

Sauté the leek rings in melted butter for 3 minutes. Add the wine and reduce slightly. Stir in the cream and vegetable broth and simmer for 5 minutes. Blend in the saffron and cheese and season. **Good with fussili.**

Per portion ca. 125 kcal/525 kJ
1 g P · 10 g F · 3 g C

Olive oil-raisin sauce

125 ml (4.5 fl oz) olive oil · 4 sliced cloves garlic · 50 g (2 oz) chopped pine nuts · 50 g (2 oz) raisins, rinsed · 3 tbsp chopped parsley

Sauté the garlic in the hot oil until translucent. Add the pine nuts and sauté a little longer, then stir in the raisins and parsley. **Good with spaghetti and macaroni.**

Per portion ca. 388 kcal/1628 kJ
4 g P · 38 g F · 10 g C

Mushroom cream sauce

2 tbsp olive oil · 1 finely chopped onion · 750 g (1 lb 10 oz) coarsely chopped mushrooms · 200 ml (7 fl oz) cream · 2 tbsp soy sauce · salt · black pepper

Heat the oil and sauté the onion in it. Add mushrooms and sauté another 5 minutes. Stir in the cream and soy sauce and simmer briefly. Salt and pepper to taste. **Good with fettuccine and penne.**

Per portion ca. 233 kcal/977 kJ
7 g P · 22 g F · 4 g C

Sauce with blue cheese

250 ml (9 fl oz) cream · 125 ml (4.5 fl oz) vegetable broth · 125 g (4.5 oz) blue cheese · 1/4 tsp black pepper · 1 tbsp Cognac

Bring the cream and vegetable broth to a boil in a pot and reduce by one third. Add the cheese and stir until melted. Season with the pepper and Cognac. **Good with tortellini, gnocchi, spaghetti.**

Per portion ca. 303 kcal/1270 kJ
8 g P · 29 g F · 3 g C

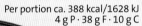

Pasta sauces

Beetroot-ricotta sauce

60 g (2 oz) butter · 300 g (10 oz) puréed beetroot · 200 g (7 oz) ricotta · 100 ml (3 fl oz) cream · 100 g (3.5 oz) grated parmesan cheese · salt · black pepper

Melt the butter in a pot and sauté the puréed beetroot in it. Stir in the ricotta and cream and bring to the boil. Add the parmesan while stirring and season with salt and pepper. **Good with ravioli and tortellini.**

Per portion ca. 408 kcal/1712 kJ
16 g P · 35 g F · 8 g C

Cold yoghurt sauce

50 g (2 oz) chopped salad gherkins · 4 tbsp chopped parsley · 2 tbsp chopped tarragon · 4 skinned and cubed tomatoes · 2 tbsp chopped capers · 2 mild green jalapeño peppers, chopped · 500 g (17 oz) plain full-cream yoghurt · salt · black pepper · pinch cayenne

Combine all ingredients in order, stirring in the yoghurt last. Season and serve immediately. **Good with farfalle, fussili and pappardelle.**

Per portion ca. 128 kcal/539 kJ
6 g P · 6 g F · 12 g C

Cheese and cream sauce

1 egg yolk · 100 ml (3 fl oz) cream · 500 ml (17 fl oz) basic light sauce (see p. 9) · 75 g (2.5 oz) each grated parmesan and Gruyère cheeses · 1 tbsp lemon juice · salt · pepper · nutmeg

Blend the egg yolk with the cream and mix into the light sauce. Heat without boiling. Strain through a sieve and stir in the cheeses, letting them melt. Season with the lemon juice and spices. **Good with all types of pasta.**

Per portion ca. 343 kcal/1439 kJ
14 g P · 26 g F · 14 g C

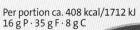

Thyme cream sauce

2 tbsp butter · 1 onion · 1 clove garlic · 1/2 tbsp flour · 125 ml (4.5 fl oz) each white wine, milk · 250 g (9 oz) whipping cream · 1/2 bunch thyme, chopped · salt · white pepper · 1 pinch cayenne · 1 tsp lemon juice

Melt the butter. Chop and sauté the onion and garlic. Add the flour, making a roux, then stir in the wine. Add the milk and cream. Simmer for 10 minutes. Fold in the thyme, then season to taste with the spices and lemon juice. **Good with ravioli.**

Per portion ca. 275 kcal/1155 kJ
3 g P · 24 g F · 7 g C

Spinach cream sauce

2 tbsp olive oil · 1 chopped onion · 1 crushed garlic clove · 500 g (17 oz) freshly rinsed spinach · 200 ml (7 fl oz) cream · 50 g (2 oz) grated parmesan cheese · salt · pepper · nutmeg

Heat the oil and sauté the onion and garlic in it. Add spinach and cook until limp. Stir in the cream and allow the sauce to reduce somewhat. Stir in the cheese and season. **Good with spaghetti, tagliatelle and fettuccine.**

Per portion ca. 285 kcal/1197 kJ
8 g P · 26 g F · 5 g C

Morel cream sauce

2 finely chopped shallots · 40 g (1.5 oz) butter · 100 g (3.5 oz) finely chopped mushrooms · 15 g (.5 oz) dried morels, soaked in water · 6 tbsp dry white wine · 100 ml (3 fl oz) cream · salt · white pepper

Sauté the shallots in hot butter. Add the mushrooms and sauté. Pour in the water in which the morels soaked and the wine. Stir in the cream and morels and allow to simmer 5 minutes. Season. **Good with ravioli.**

Per portion ca. 171 kcal/716 kJ
2 g P · 16 g F · 3 g C

Pasta sauces

Minced meat sauce

100 g (3.5 oz) cubed smoked bacon · 2 onions ·
2 cloves garlic · 2 bunches vegetables for soup · 4 tbsp
olive oil · 400 g (14 oz) mixed minced meat · 1 tin diced
tomatoes (450 g/1 lb) · 2 tbsp tomato purée · 100 ml
(3 fl oz) red wine · 2 tsp dried Italian herbs · salt · pepper ·
paprika

Render the bacon and sauté the chopped onions, garlic
and soup vegetables in the fat. Heat the oil in a second
pan and brown the mince. Add tomatoes, tomato purée
and wine. Combine the two mixtures and season well
with herbs and spices. Cook thoroughly, about 20 minutes, until sauce thickens. **Good with all types of pasta.**
Per portion ca. 603 kcal/2531 kJ · 20 g P · 55 g F · 6 g C

Sausage sauce

3 tbsp sunflower seed oil · 3 tbsp butter ·
1 chopped onion · 1 cubed carrot · 100 g (3.5 oz) chopped
celeriac · 1 red bell pepper · 150 g (5 oz) Italian sausage
(*salsicce*) · 50 ml (2 fl oz) meat broth · 2 tbsp tomato purée ·
1/2 bunch fresh basil, chopped · salt · pepper

Heat the oil and butter and sauté the onion for 4 minutes,
then add the carrot and celeriac. Trim and finely slice the
red pepper. Thinly slice the sausage. Add the pepper,
sausage, broth and tomato purée to the vegetables, bring
to the boil and simmer 5 minutes. Stir in the basil and
season to taste with salt and pepper. **Good with penne,
rigatoni.**
Per portion ca. 217 kcal/911 kJ · 8 g P · 19 g F · 4 g C

Liver sauce

50 g (2 oz) butter · 2 chopped onions · 300 g
(10 oz) beef liver · 2 tbsp flour · 1 bay leaf · 1 sage leaf ·
125 ml (4.5 fl oz) red wine · 1 tbsp chopped fresh thyme ·
salt · pepper

Heat the butter in a pan and sauté the onion in it. Wash,
dry and cube the liver. Dust with flour and add to the
onion along with the bay and sage leaves. Sauté well
while stirring, then pour in the red wine and allow the
mixture to cook for about 4 minutes. Remove the bay and
sage leaves, and stir in the thyme. Season to taste with
salt and pepper. **Good with garganelli and wholegrain
spaghetti.**

Per portion ca. 242 kcal/1016 kJ · 16 g P · 14 g F · 9 g C

Sauce with chicken breast

1 crushed clove garlic · 2 tbsp olive oil · 1 chopped
green bell pepper · 500 g (17 oz) chopped chicken breast ·
250 g (9 oz) small mushrooms · 100 ml (3 fl oz) white wine ·
250 ml (9 fl oz) cream · 100 g (3.5 oz) grated pecorino
cheese · salt · pepper

Sauté the garlic in the oil. Add the pepper and chicken
breast and cook for 15 minutes while stirring. Clean and
dry the mushrooms and add them. Pour in the wine, bring
to the boil and simmer for 3 minutes, then remove from
the heat and stir in the cream and cheese. Season the
sauce. **Good with penne, rigatoni, fussili and macaroni.**

Per portion ca. 460 kcal/1932 kJ · 40 g P · 30 g F · 5 g C

Pasta sauces

Nut sauce

150 g (5 oz) ricotta cheese · 125 ml (4.5 fl oz) olive oil · 200 g (7 oz) ground hazelnuts · 2 tbsp chopped fresh marjoram · 75 g (2.5 oz) grated pecorino cheese · salt · pepper

Pour the ricotta cheese into a food processor and gradually add the olive oil until the mixture is creamy. Add nuts, marjoram and pecorino cheese, and season with salt and pepper. **Good with tagliatelle and fettuccine.**

Per portion ca. 685 kcal/2877 kJ
15 g P · 68 g F · 6 g C

Green and red pepper sauce

2 tbsp olive oil · 1 chopped onion · 1 green and 1 red bell pepper, both chopped finely · 4 eggs · salt · white pepper · 1 pinch cayenne

Heat the olive oil and sauté the onions and peppers in it. Whisk together the eggs and spices. Blend the pepper mixture together with the egg mixture and serve on top of hot noodles. **Good with farfalle.**

Per portion ca. 169 kcal/709 kJ
9 g P · 13 g F · 4 g C

Bacon cream sauce

1 tbsp olive oil · 250 g (9 oz) ham bacon, cut into small strips · 4 hard-cooked eggs · 50 ml (2 fl oz) cream · 100 g (3.5 oz) grated parmesan cheese · salt · white pepper

Heat the oil and cook the bacon in it. Chop the eggs and stir into the cream with the parmesan cheese, blending well. Season with salt and pepper. Mix with the bacon. **Good with spaghetti.**

Per portion ca. 363 kcal/1523 kJ
29 g P · 27 g F · 1 g C

Ham cream sauce

Wine and herbs sauce

Maize cream sauce

120 g (4 oz) Parma ham · 80 g (2.75 oz) cooked ham · 60 g (2 oz) butter · 250 ml (9 fl oz) cream · 2 tbsp basic light sauce (see p. 9) · salt · pepper · nutmeg · 80 g (2.75 oz) grated parmesan cheese

Chop all the ham and briefly sauté it in the butter. Pour in the cream, stir in light sauce and cook until thickened. Season with salt, pepper and nutmeg, then stir in the cheese. Simmer another 5 minutes. **Good with pappardelle, macaroni and penne.**

Per portion ca. 540 kcal/2268 kJ
20 g P · 51 g F · 3 g C

6 tbsp olive oil · 1 chopped onion · 2 chopped garlic cloves · 1 bunch fresh mixed herbs, chopped · 2 sage leaves, chopped · 1/2 tsp chopped rosemary · 1 pulverised bay leaf · 125 ml (4.5 fl oz) dry white wine · 1 container crème fraîche · salt

Sauté the onion and garlic in the heated oil. Add all the herbs and pour in the wine. Simmer for 15 minutes, then stir in the crème fraîche and season with salt. **Good with all types of pasta.**

Per portion ca. 209 kcal/878 kJ
1 g P · 20 g F · 2 g C

1 chopped onion · 1 chopped garlic clove · 50 g (2 oz) butter · 1/2 bunch flat-leaf parsley, chopped · 200 ml (7 fl oz) cream · 1 tin sweet maize (280 g/ 10 oz), drained · salt · white pepper · nutmeg

Purée the onion and garlic, then sauté in the heated butter. Add the parsley and cream and bring to the boil. Stir in the maize, heating it in the sauce. Season with salt, pepper and nutmeg. **Good with farfalle.**

Per portion ca. 478 kcal/2006 kJ
8 g P · 28 g F · 49 g C

Pasta sauces

Tofu sauce

3 tbsp sunflower seed oil · 300 g (10 oz) green
and red bell peppers, diced · 100 g (3.5 oz) cubed onion ·
400 ml (14 fl oz) vegetable broth · 8 tbsp soy sauce · 250 g
(9 oz) tofu, cubed · 2 tbsp olive oil · 1 bunch basil, chopped ·
3 tbsp basic tomato sauce (see p. 9) · salt · pepper

Heat the oil and sauté the peppers and onion in it. Pour in
the broth and soy sauce and simmer for 20 minutes.
Sauté the tofu in hot olive oil. Add the basil to the sauce,
thicken with the basic tomato sauce and season. Stir in
the tofu. **Good with spaghetti and spaghettini.**

Per portion ca. 273 kcal/1145 kJ · 13 g P · 22 g F · 6 g C

Sauce with fish and mint

1 chopped garlic clove · 3 tbsp olive oil · 2 tomatoes, cubed · 15 g (.5 oz) chopped mint · 1 tbsp red
wine vinegar · 2 tbsp basic tomato sauce (see p. 9) · salt ·
pepper · 500 g (17 oz) chopped fish fillet (such as
swordfish) · 1 tsp grated orange peel

Sauté the garlic in the hot olive oil. Add the cubed tomato
and simmer for 15 minutes. Then add the mint, vinegar
and basic tomato sauce. Season with salt and pepper. Stir
in the fish cubes and stew in the sauce for 5 minutes.
Flavour with the orange peel. **Good with macaroni.**

Per portion ca. 237 kcal/995 kJ · 26 g P · 14 g F · 2 g C

Courgette-sage sauce

6 tbsp olive oil · 2 chopped cloves garlic · 500 g
(17 oz) courgettes, halved lengthwise and sliced · 6 sage
leaves, cut into strips · 50 g (2 oz) vegetable broth · 100 ml
(3 fl oz) basic light sauce (see p. 9) · 8 tbsp dry white wine ·
2 tbsp marinated green peppercorns · salt

Heat the olive oil and cook the garlic in it until translucent. Add the courgettes and sage and cook briefly. Pour
in the broth, light sauce and wine and allow to reduce
somewhat. Stir in the peppercorns and season with salt.
Good with pappardelle, ravioli, lasagne.

Per portion ca. 212 kcal/892 kJ · 3 g P · 20 g F · 6 g C

Aubergine sauce

3 tbsp butter · 100 g (3.5 oz) aubergine, cut into
cubes and drizzled with lemon juice · 100 g (3.5 oz) green
and red bell pepper, diced · 2 green onions, cut into rings ·
1/2 bunch parsley, chopped · 400 ml (14 fl oz) beef broth ·
4 tbsp Grappa · 2 tbsp crème fraîche · 3 tbsp basic light
sauce (see p. 9)

Heat the butter in a pot and sauté the vegetables and
parsley in it. Fill the pot with the beef broth and allow to
simmer for a few minutes. Stir in the Grappa and crème
fraîche and thicken with the basic light sauce. Season.
Good with all types of pasta.

Per portion ca. 140 kcal/590 kJ · 4 g P · 11 g F · 6 g C

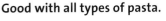

Pasta sauces

Garlic sauce with parsley

1 large clove garlic · 5 tbsp olive oil ·
2 tbsp chopped fresh parsley · 1/4 tsp
salt · 1/4 tsp pepper

Peel and chop the garlic clove finely.
Heat the oil in a pot and sauté the
garlic in it until light golden brown.
Take the pot from the heat and stir in
the parsley. Season with salt and
pepper. **Good with spaghetti,
tagliatelle and spaghettini.**

Per portion ca. 136 kcal/572 kJ
22 g P · 15 g F · 1 g C

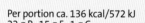

Truffle sauce

3 cloves garlic, chopped · 3 fresh
anchovy fillets · 6 tbsp olive oil · 120 g
(4 oz) black truffles · 150 ml (5 fl oz)
cream · salt · pepper

Purée the cloves of garlic and the
anchovy fillets. Heat the oil and
sauté the garlic-anchovy purée in it.
Pound the truffles and add to the
mix, along with the cream, while
stirring. Season to taste with salt and
pepper. **Good with all types of pasta.**

Per portion ca. 363 kcal/1523 kJ
18 g P · 31 g F · 4 g C

Tuna fish sauce

2 tbsp olive oil · 2 cloves garlic,
chopped · 200 g (7 oz) peeled, diced
tomatoes · 150 g (5 oz) mussels
(tinned) · 325 g (11 oz) tuna fish
(tinned) · salt · pepper · 2 tbsp
chopped parsley

Heat the oil and sauté garlic. Add
tomatoes and cook 5 minutes. Add
the mussels, tuna fish and some
liquid from the mussels and bring
to the boil. Season and stir in the
parsley. **Good with spaghetti,
macaroni, penne.**

Per portion ca. 273 kcal/1145 kJ
22 g P · 19 g F · 4 g C

Salmon cream sauce

3 tbsp olive oil · 2 cloves garlic · 60 g (2 oz) chopped black olives · 100 g (3.5 oz) salmon, cubed · 100 ml (3 fl oz) cream · 300 g (10 oz) puréed tomatoes · salt · pepper · 1/2 tsp chopped oregano · 1 tsp chopped dill

Heat the olive oil and sauté the chopped garlic in it. Add the olives and salmon, sautéing 3 minutes more. Stir in the cream and tomato purée. Bring to the boil and season with the herbs and spices. **Good with fusilli.**

Per portion ca. 253 kcal/1061 kJ
6 g P · 24 g F · 4 g C

Mussel sauce

3 tbsp olive oil · 1 chopped onion · 1 clove garlic, chopped · 4 tomatoes, peeled and cubed · 2 kg (4 lb 6 oz) cooked blue mussels, without shells · salt · black pepper

Heat the olive oil and sauté the onion and garlic in it. Add the tomato cubes, season and simmer until the sauce thickens. Stir in the mussels and cook until well heated. **Good with spaghetti and tagliatelle.**

Per portion ca. 435 kcal/1827 kJ
50 g P · 16 g F · 22 g C

Clam sauce

24 clams · 125 ml (4.5 fl oz) white wine · 4 tbsp olive oil · 1 clove garlic, finely chopped · 1/4 tsp chopped chilli · 2 tbsp chopped parsley · salt · white pepper · 3 tbsp basic light sauce (see p. 9)

Cook the clams in the wine, remove from their shells and chop. Strain the broth. Heat the oil and sauté the garlic and chilli. Add the clams, clam broth, basic light sauce and parsley and heat through. Season. **Good with spaghetti, buccatini.**

Per portion ca. 595 kcal/2499 kJ
67 g P · 17 g F · 37 g C

Pasta sauces

Mozzarella sauce

3 tbsp olive oil · 1 shallot · 1 clove garlic · 250 g (9 oz) peeled, cubed tomatoes · 2 tbsp balsamic vinegar · 200 ml (7 fl oz) red wine · 200 ml (7 fl oz) vegetable broth · 100 g (3.5 oz) mozzarella · 3 tbsp basic tomato sauce (see p. 9) · 1 bunch fresh basil, chopped · salt · pepper

Heat the olive oil. Chop the shallots and garlic. Sauté both with the tomatoes, then let simmer. Add the vinegar, wine and broth. Cut mozzarella in strips and stir into the sauce. Allow to cook a few moments. Thicken with the tomato sauce, stir in basil and season. **Good with lasagne, gnocchi and spaghetti.**

Per portion ca. 221 kcal/929 kJ · 6 g P · 16 g F · 5 g C

Mackerel-prawn sauce

2 tbsp butter · 100 g (3.5 oz) smoked mackerel fillets, cubed · 100 g (3.5 oz) cooked shrimp, drained · 2 tbsp lemon juice · 400 ml (14 fl oz) fish broth · 3 tbsp basic light sauce (see p. 9) · salt · pepper · curry powder · nutmeg

Melt the butter in a pot and briefly heat the mackerel fillets and shrimp in it. Pour in the lemon juice and fish broth and allow the sauce to cook for a short while. Thicken with the basic light sauce and season to taste with the spices. **Good with rigatoni, buccatini, macaroni.**

Per portion ca. 144 kcal/604 kJ · 12 g P · 10 g F · 3 g C

Cold vegetable sauce

1 yellow bell pepper · 1/2 red chilli · 1/2 long cucumber, seeds removed · 400 g (14 oz) tomatoes, skins and stems removed · 1 onion, chopped · 2 cloves garlic · 4 tbsp bread crumbs · 4 tbsp olive oil · 1/2 bunch basil · salt · black pepper · 2 tbsp red wine vinegar

Place all ingredients except the spices and vinegar in a food processor and purée. Season the sauce with salt, pepper and vinegar. **Good with all types of pasta.**

Per portion ca. 162 kcal/680 kJ · 3 g P · 13 g F · 9 g C

Seafood sauce

4 tbsp olive oil · 250 g (9 oz) frozen seafood, thawed · 1 onion, chopped · 2 cloves garlic, chopped · 1/2 bunch tarragon · 200 ml (7 fl oz) white wine · 400 ml (14 fl oz) lobster stock · 1/4 tsp grated lime peel · 2 tbsp cream · 2 tbsp basic brown sauce (see p. 9) · salt · pepper

Heat the oil and sauté the seafood, onion and garlic in it. Stir in the tarragon. Pour in the white wine and stock. Allow to cook for a short time. Stir in the grated lime peel and the cream, then thicken with the basic brown sauce. Season. **Good with shell pasta and black fettuccine.**

Per portion ca. 247 kcal/1037 kJ · 8 g P · 19 g F · 5 g C

Pasta sauces

Coriander sauce with ginger

2 bunches coriander leaf, chopped ·
1 tbsp fresh chopped ginger · 1 mild
chilli, finely chopped · 100 ml (3 fl oz)
coconut milk · 1 tbsp lemon juice ·
1 tsp sugar · 50 ml (2 fl oz) safflower
oil · 2 cloves garlic, peeled · 2 tbsp
lime juice · salt

Purée all ingredients except the
garlic, lime juice and salt in a food
processor. Crush the garlic and add to
the mixture. Season with lime juice
and salt. **Good with penne or ravioli.**

Per portion ca. 140 kcal/588 kJ
1 g P · 14 g F · 4 g C

Fennel sauce with scampi

1 tbsp butter · 2 bulbs fennel, cut into
strips · 1 clove garlic, finely chopped ·
1 tsp turmeric · 100 ml (3 fl oz) white
wine · 250 g (9 oz) scampi (prawns),
cooked and peeled · 100 g (3.5 oz)
butter, cut into cubes · 4 tbsp sour
cream · salt · black pepper

Sauté the fennel and garlic in hot
butter. Add the turmeric and wine,
and after 5 minutes the prawns. Stir
in the butter cubes and sour cream.
Season. **Good with fussili and penne.**

Per portion ca. 315 kcal/1323 kJ
14 g P · 25 g F · 5 g C

Vegetable-peanut sauce

100 g (3.5 oz) peanut butter · 4 tbsp
soy sauce · 2 tbsp sweet soy sauce ·
1 tbsp fruit vinegar · a few splashes
Tabasco Sauce · 300 g (10 oz) cooked
broccoli · 250 g (9 oz) cooked carrots,
cut into strips

Stir the peanut butter together with
125 ml (4.5 fl oz) hot water, season
with soy sauces, vinegar and Tabasco
Sauce. Mix in the cooked vegetables.
**Good with spaghetti and fried
noodles.**

Per portion ca. 178 kcal/748 kJ
10 g P · 13 g F · 6 g C

Horseradish-orange sauce

Juice of 1 orange · 300 g (10 oz) sour cream · 5 tbsp oil · 8 tbsp tomato purée · 4 tbsp brandy · 2 tsp freshly grated horseradish · salt · pepper · cayenne

Blend the orange juice, sour cream, oil, tomato purée, brandy and horseradish together well. Add savoury seasoning with the spices. **Good with baked and fried noodles.**

Per portion ca. 255 kcal/1071 kJ
3 g P · 23 g F · 7 g C

Carrot cream sauce

2 tbsp oil · 4 green onions, chopped · 500 g (17 oz) carrots, cut into small cubes · 200 ml (7 fl oz) vegetable broth · 60 g (2 oz) crème fraîche · pinch cayenne · salt

Heat the oil and sauté the onion in it. Add the carrots and sauté briefly. Pour in the broth and cook until soft. Purée the carrots, stir into the broth with the crème fraîche and season to taste with cayenne and salt. **Good with spaghettini and baked noodle nests.**

Per portion ca. 144 kcal/606 kJ
2 g P · 12 g F · 7 g C

Leek sauce with bacon

2 tbsp butter · 50 g (2 oz) cubed bacon · 100 g (3.5 oz) leeks, cut into rings · 350 ml (12 fl oz) vegetable broth · 4 tbsp wine vinegar · 1/2 bunch mixed herbs, chopped · 3 tbsp basic brown sauce (see p. 9) · salt · pepper

Heat the butter and render the bacon in it. Add leek and sauté together for 5 minutes. Pour on the broth, bring to the boil and let thicken. Stir in the vinegar and herbs. Thicken with the basic sauce and season. **Good with penne and rigatoni.**

Per portion ca. 98 kcal/412 kJ
4 g P · 8 g F · 3 g C

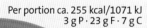

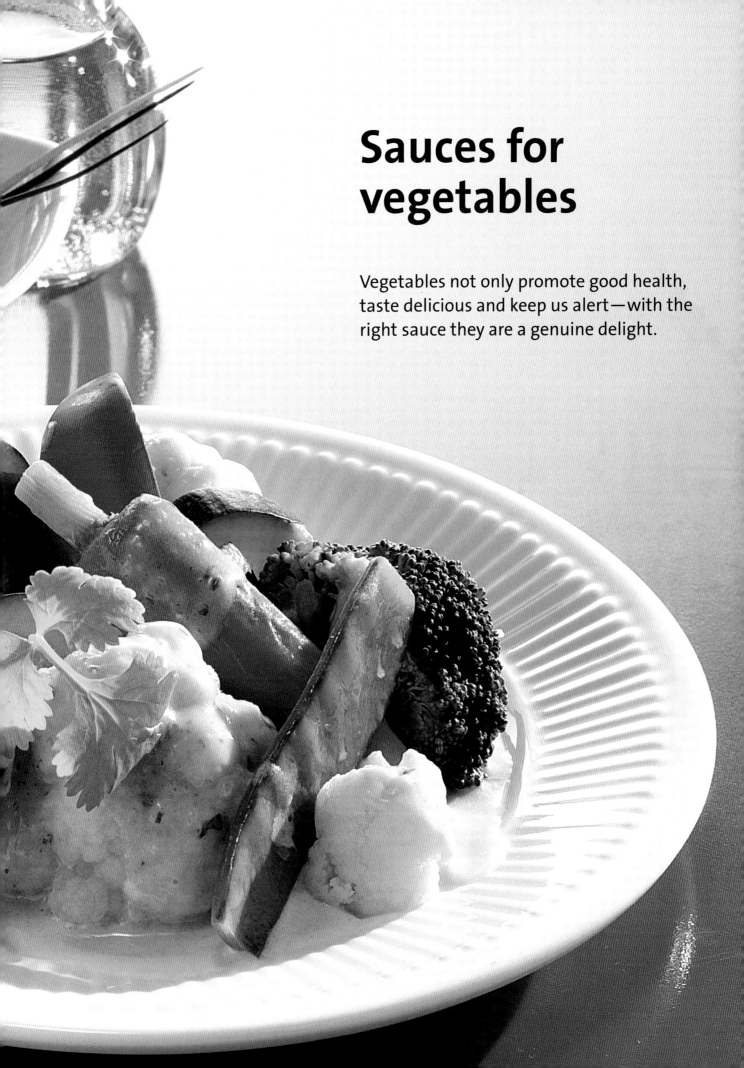

Sauces for vegetables

Vegetables not only promote good health, taste delicious and keep us alert—with the right sauce they are a genuine delight.

Sauces for vegetables

Cold sour cream sauce

200 ml (7 fl oz) sour cream

100 ml (3 fl oz) yoghurt

150 ml (5 fl oz) cream

1–2 tsp lemon juice

1/2 tsp cayenne

salt

white pepper

1. Stir together the sour cream, yoghurt and cream.

2. Season to taste with lemon juice and the spices and refrigerate for 10 minutes.

Good with roasted and boiled potatoes.

Per portion ca. 203 kcal/853 kJ
4 g P · 19 g F · 5 g C

Variation 1

Prepare the cream sauce according to the basic recipe, adding to it 2 puréed hard-cooked egg yolks, 1 tsp mustard and 1 tbsp fresh chopped herbs. **Good with cauliflower and broccoli.**

Per portion ca. 250 kcal/1050 kJ
8 g P · 22 g F · 5 g C

Variation 2

Prepare the cream sauce as in the basic recipe, but without the lemon juice. Add 100 g (3.5 oz) finely chopped matjes herring fillets or 60 g (2 oz) black caviar. **Good with baked potatoes and kohlrabi.**

Per portion ca. 288 kcal/1208 kJ
11 g P · 24 g F · 6 g C

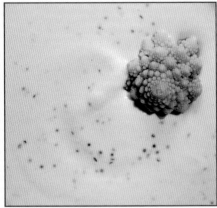

Variation 3

Prepare the cream sauce as in the basic recipe, but substitute 1 tsp curry powder and 1/2 tsp turmeric for the lemon juice. Stir in 1 tsp chopped fresh coriander leaf. **Good with snow peas and carrots.**

Per portion ca. 210 kcal/881 kJ
4 g P · 19 g F · 6 g C

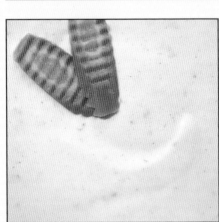

Variation 4

Add 2 tbsp tomato purée to the cream sauce. Instead of the lemon juice, add a shot of Worcestershire sauce or soy sauce. **Good with courgettes and aubergines.**

Per portion ca. 206 kcal/866 kJ
4 g P · 19 g F · 6 g C

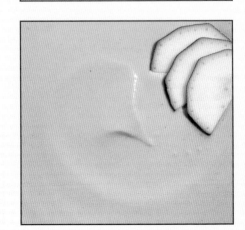

Sauces for vegetables

Caper sauce

1 egg yolk · 1 tbsp mustard · 120 ml (4 fl oz) sunflower seed oil · 4 tbsp capers · 1 hard-cooked egg · 1/2 bunch parsley, chopped · salt · black pepper · 2 tbsp lemon juice

Combine the egg yolk and mustard and slowly mix in the oil. Finely chop 3 tbsp of the finely and add to the sauce with the whole capers. Peel and chop the egg. Add to the sauce with the parsley. Season with salt, pepper and lemon juice. **Good with cooked vegetables as a cold sauce.**

Per portion ca. 333 kcal/1397 kJ
3 g P · 35 g F · 3 g C

Tarragon-gin sauce

1 onion, chopped · 2 cloves garlic, crushed · 2 tbsp olive oil · 100 g (3.5 oz) pheasant breast, cubed · 1/2 bunch tarragon, chopped · 400 ml (14 fl oz) poultry stock · 3 tbsp basic tomato sauce (see p. 9) · 1 shot gin · salt · pepper · ground paprika

Sauté the onion and garlic in hot oil, add the pheasant breast cubes and sauté for 5 minutes. Add the tarragon and stock and let simmer for a while. Thicken with the basic tomato sauce and season with the gin and spices. **Good with grilled and roasted maize.**

Per portion ca. 195 kcal/817 kJ
13 g P · 15 g F · 3 g C

Lemon cream sauce

8 leaves each mint and lemon balm · 1/2 bunch basil, chopped · 1/2 tsp salt · 4 tbsp lemon juice · 200 ml (7 fl oz) cream · 3 tbsp basic light sauce (see p. 9)

Mix the herbs, salt and lemon juice and let steep for 20 minutes. Pour the juice off and stir it into the cream. Thicken the sauce with the basic light sauce and warm without boiling. Stir in the herbs. **Good with artichokes and asparagus.**

Per portion ca. 160 kcal/669 kJ
2 g P · 16 g F · 4 g C

Yoghurt-herb sauce

100 g (3.5 oz) mayonnaise · 100 g (3.5 oz) yoghurt · 50 ml (2 fl oz) cream · 3 hard-cooked eggs · 2 bunches mixed herbs, chopped · 1 shallot, chopped finely · salt · pepper · 1 pinch sugar

Mix the mayonnaise, yoghurt and cream. Peel and chop the eggs. Stir into the mayonnaise along with the herbs and shallot. Season to taste with salt, pepper and sugar. **Good as a dip for raw and cooked vegetables.**

Per portion ca. 318 kcal/1334 kJ
8 g P · 31 g F · 4 g C

Sauces for vegetables

Bagna cauda

8 anchovy fillets · 2 cloves garlic, crushed · 375 ml (13 fl oz) cream · 100 g (3.5 oz) butter

Wash, dry and finely purée the anchovies. In a saucepan, heat the cream and reduce it by half. Heat the butter in a fry pan and sauté the anchovy purée and garlic in it. Stir in the cream with a whisk, making sure the sauce does not boil. **Good as a hot dip for raw vegetables.**

Per portion ca. 610 kcal/2562 kJ
33 g P · 53 g F · 3 g C

Herb sauce

2 tbsp butter · 2 onions · 2 cloves garlic · 1/2 bunch herbs, chopped · 2 tbsp mustard · 400 ml (14 fl oz) vegetable broth · 3 tbsp basic light sauce (see p. 9) · 2 tbsp crème fraîche · salt · pepper · lemon juice

Chop the onions and garlic. Sauté them in the melted butter. Add the herbs, sauté briefly, then add mustard and broth and reduce slightly. Add the basic light sauce, season to taste and stir in lemon juice. **Good with carrots.**

Per portion ca. 97 kcal/408 kJ
1 g P · 8 g F · 4 g C

Turmeric sauce

2 tbsp oil · 2 onions, chopped · 3 tomatoes, peeled and chopped · 100 g (3.5 oz) ground cashew nuts · 1 tsp each turmeric, chilli powder, ground coriander and salt · 100 g (3.5 oz) full-fat yoghurt · 500 ml (17 fl oz) vegetable broth

Sauté the onions and tomatoes in hot oil. Blend the cashews with the spices and yoghurt, then add to the sauce. Pour in the broth and simmer 10 minutes. **Good with cauliflower and okra.**

Per portion ca. 231 kcal/968 kJ
7 g P · 17 g F · 13 g C

Sherry sauce

2 tbsp olive oil · 1 onion, chopped · 2 cloves garlic, crushed · 200 ml (7 fl oz) each mushroom stock and sherry · 3 tbsp basic tomato sauce (see p. 9) · 2 tbsp crème fraîche · salt · pepper · paprika · 1/2 bunch parsley, chopped

Sauté the onion and garlic in hot oil. Pour in the stock and sherry and reduce slightly. Thicken with the basic tomato sauce and crème fraîche and season with spices. Stir in the parsley. **Good with Chinese cabbage.**

Per portion ca. 147 kcal/616 kJ
1 g P · 9 g F · 3 g C

Beer sauce

4 egg yolks · salt · 375 ml (13 fl oz) *altbier* (brown or dark ale will substitute) · black pepper · cayenne · a bit of lemon juice

Beat the egg yolks with the salt until foamy and place over a hot but not boiling double boiler. Pour in the *altbier* or ale while whisking continuously until the sauce is thick and creamy. Season the sauce with spices and lemon juice. **Good with peppers, courgettes and aubergines.**

Per portion ca. 158 kcal/664 kJ
4 g P · 7 g F · 15 g C

Lemon sauce

1 tbsp Dijon mustard · 3 egg yolks · juice of 2 lemons · 8 tbsp sunflower seed oil · salt · pepper

Blend the mustard and egg yolks together well, then gradually add the lemon juice. Finally drizzle the oil in slowly. Work the mixture into a creamy sauce while whisking. Season to taste with pepper and salt. **Good with vegetable salads.**

Per portion ca. 154 kcal/647 kJ
3 g P · 15 g F · 2 g C

Sauces for vegetables

Garlic-potato sauce

2 cloves garlic · 1 tsp salt · 125 g (4.5 oz) boiled potatoes · 1 egg yolk · olive oil · 250 ml (9 fl oz) cream · 2 tbsp lemon juice · pepper

Peel the garlic and crush with the salt. Peel and cube the potatoes. Purée potatoes and garlic in a food processor. Gradually add the egg yolk and cream. Pour in just as much olive oil as the potato mixture absorbs. Season to taste with lemon juice, pepper and additional salt. **Good with roasted courgettes, aubergines and mushrooms.**

Per portion ca. 232 kcal/974 kJ · 3 g P · 21 g F · 8 g C

Asian sauce

3 tbsp olive oil · 3 green onions, cut into rings · 200 g (7 oz) chicken breast, cut into strips · 15 g (1 oz) Chinese mushrooms, soaked · 300 ml (10 fl oz) chicken broth · 5 tbsp rice wine · 3 tbsp basic tomato sauce (see p. 9) · salt · pepper · sweet soy sauce

Sauté the green onions in the oil, then add the chicken breast. Briefly sauté the drained mushrooms in this mixture. Stir in the water they soaked in, the broth and rice wine and allow to reduce some. Thicken with the basic tomato sauce and season. **Good with green beans.**

Per portion ca. 263 kcal/1103 kJ · 26 g P · 13 g F · 11 g C

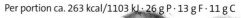

Sweet and sour sauce

350 ml (12 fl oz) apricot juice · 1 peeled and cubed papaya · juice and the grated peel of 1 lime · 1 tsp turmeric · 1/2 bunch coriander leaf, chopped · 3 tbsp chopped pistachios · 3 tbsp basic light sauce (see p. 9) · salt · pepper

Heat up apricot juice, papaya, lime juice and peel and stir in the turmeric. Allow to reduce for 10 minutes. Stir in the coriander and pistachios, then thicken with the basic light sauce. Season to taste. **Good with beetroot.**

Per portion ca. 345 kcal/1449 kJ · 28 g P · 16 g F · 22 g C

Meat sauce

2 tbsp herb butter · 2 onions, chopped · 1 clove garlic, finely chopped · 100 g (3.5 oz) cubed pork roast · 350 ml (12 fl) veal stock · 1/2 bunch sage, chopped · 2 tbsp crème fraîche · 3 tbsp basic brown sauce (see p. 9) · salt · pepper

Sauté the onions and garlic in the herb butter. Add and brown the pork roast cubes. Pour the veal stock into the pan and reduce somewhat. Stir in the crème fraîche and thicken with the basic brown sauce. Season. **Good with celeriac and carrots.**

Per portion ca. 152 kcal/638 kJ · 13 g P · 10 g F · 4 g C

Sauces for vegetables

Chervil sauce

3 tbsp olive oil · 1 bunch chervil, chopped · 1 red chilli, finely chopped · 400 ml (14 fl oz) vegetable broth · 3 tbsp basic brown sauce (see p. 9) · salt · pepper · paprika

Heat the oil and sauté the chervil and chopped chilli in it. Pour in the vegetable broth and allow the sauce to reduce somewhat. Thicken with the basic brown sauce and season to taste with the spices. **Good with fresh peas and soy bean sprouts.**

Per portion ca. 120 kcal/502 kJ
1 g P · 12 g F · 2 g C

Wine sauce

1 tbsp butter · 2 chopped shallots · 375 ml (13 fl oz) dry Riesling wine · 125 g (4.5 oz) chilled butter · salt · white pepper · a bit of cayenne · Worcestershire sauce

Heat the butter and sauté the shallots in it. Pour in the wine and allow to reduce somewhat. Beat the chilled butter into the sauce firmly with a whisk until the sauce becomes creamy. Season to taste with the spices and Worcestershire sauce. **Good with chicory and endive.**

Per portion ca. 330 kcal/1386 kJ
1 g P · 28 g F · 4 g C

Cress sauce

2 tbsp butter · 2 carrots, cubed · 1 onion, chopped · 1 tbsp soy sauce · 100 ml (3 fl oz) white wine · 200 ml (7 fl oz) veal stock · 3 hard-cooked eggs, chopped · 3 tbsp basic light sauce (see p. 9) · 1 small box cress · salt · pepper

Heat the butter and sauté the carrots and onions in it. Add the soy sauce, wine and stock and simmer. Purée the sauce and stir in the egg. Blend in the light sauce and cress. Season. **Good with snow peas and green beans.**

Per portion ca. 173 kcal/727 kJ
12 g P · 11 g F · 4 g C

Mortadella dip

3 tbsp olive oil · 1 onion, chopped · 250 g (9 oz) Mortadella, cut into strips · 400 ml (14 fl oz) beef broth · 1/2 bunch each tarragon and thyme, chopped · 3 tbsp basic light sauce (see p. 9) · salt · pepper

Heat the oil and sauté the onion in it. Add the Mortadella and continue sautéing. Pour in the beef broth, then allow the sauce to reduce somewhat. Stir in the herbs and thicken with the basic light sauce. Season. **Good with all types of cabbage.**

Per portion ca. 249 kcal/1046 kJ
17 g P · 18 g F · 4 g C

Shrimp sauce

2 tbsp butter · 1 chopped shallot · 150 g (5 oz) shrimp · 2 tbsp lemon juice · 400 ml (14 fl oz) lobster stock · 1/2 bunch dill, chopped · 3 tbsp basic light sauce (see p. 9) · salt · white pepper · cayenne

Sauté the shallot in the heated butter. Add the shrimp and continue cooking. Pour in the lemon juice and lobster stock and allow the sauce to reduce somewhat. Stir in the dill and thicken with the basic light sauce. Season. **Good with fennel and chicory.**

Per portion ca. 118 kcal/495 kJ
10 g P · 7 g F · 4 g C

Quince sauce

6 tbsp butter · 100 g (3.5 oz) chopped walnuts · 60 g (2 oz) quince jelly · 1 tbsp balsamic vinegar · 125 ml (4.5 fl oz) Madeira · 250 ml (9 fl oz) vegetable broth · 125 ml (4.5 fl oz) red wine

Heat the butter and toast the walnuts in it. Add the quince jelly and allow everything to caramelise. Pour in the vinegar, Madeira, broth and red wine and let the sauce reduce somewhat. **Good with potato dishes.**

Per portion ca. 378 kcal/1586 kJ
5 g P · 31 g F · 16 g C

Sauces for vegetables

Mornay sauce

3 tbsp béchamel sauce (see p. 10) · 100 g (3.5 oz) cream · 30 g (1 oz) freshly grated Emmentaler cheese · 30 g (1 oz) freshly grated parmesan cheese · 25 g (1 oz) chilled butter

Prepare the béchamel sauce (see p. 10). Blend in the cream and then the two types of cheese, stirring as they melt. Add the chilled butter, small shavings at a time, until the sauce is creamy. **Good with broccoli, asparagus and black salsify.**

Per portion ca. 203 kcal/852 kJ
6 g P · 19 g F · 2 g C

Chilli sauce

2 tbsp garlic butter · 1/2 bunch green onions, chopped · 100 g (3.5 oz) cubed chicken breast fillet · 1 red chilli, finely chopped · 100 ml (3 fl oz) white wine · 300 ml (10 fl oz) poultry stock · 3 tbsp basic tomato sauce (see p. 9) · salt · pepper

Sauté the green onions in the butter. Add the chicken meat and chilli and cook thoroughly. Pour in the white wine and stock and allow to reduce somewhat. Thicken with the tomato sauce and season. **Good with Swiss chard and bok choi.**

Per portion ca. 162 kcal/678 kJ
11 g P · 10 g F · 3 g C

Lime sauce

225 g (8 oz) yoghurt · 150 g (5 oz) crème fraîche · 1 tbsp flour · 125 ml (4.5 fl oz) vegetable broth · grated peel and juice of 1 lime · salt · pepper

Blend the yoghurt and crème fraîche in a saucepan and heat. Stir in the flour and vegetable broth and bring to the boil until the sauce thickens. Stir in the lime peel and juice and season to taste with salt and pepper. **Good with pointed cabbage.**

Per portion ca. 170 kcal/714 kJ
3 g P · 15 g F · 5 g C

Almond sauce

1 tbsp butter · 1 shallot, chopped · 100 g (3.5 oz) chopped almonds · 125 ml (4.5 fl oz) white wine · 250 ml (9 fl oz) vegetable broth · 1 tsp curry powder · 3 tbsp basic light sauce (see p. 9) · 2 tbsp crème fraîche · salt · pepper · ground cumin · lemon juice

Sauté the shallot and almonds in the butter. Add the wine and broth. Reduce slightly, then stir in curry powder. Thicken with the light sauce and season with remaining ingredients. **Good with cauliflower and kohlrabi.**

Per portion ca. 227 kcal/951 kJ
5 g P · 19 g F · 4 g C

Tahini sauce

150 g (5 oz) tahini · 400 ml (14 fl oz) vegetable broth · 1 clove garlic, chopped · 2 tbsp lime juice · 3 tbsp tomato purée · salt · pepper · Tabasco Sauce · soy sauce · 3 tbsp basic brown sauce (see p. 9)

Mix the tahini and vegetable broth and bring to the boil with the garlic and lime juice. Allow to reduce by a third. Add the tomato purée, then season and thicken with the basic brown sauce. **Good with Chinese cabbage and savoy cabbage.**

Per portion ca. 268 kcal/1123 kJ
8 g P · 21 g F · 12 g C

Tomato sauce

2 tbsp olive oil · 2 onions, chopped · 150 ml (5 fl oz) white wine · 200 ml (7 fl oz) chicken broth · 2 tbsp fruit vinegar · 1 tsp each chopped oregano and basil · 3 tbsp basic tomato sauce (see p. 9) · salt · pepper · cayenne · sugar

Heat the oil in a fry pan and sauté the onions. Add the wine, broth, vinegar and herbs. Allow to reduce somewhat. Thicken with the tomato sauce and season with the spices and sugar. **Good with aubergines and courgettes.**

Per portion ca. 190 kcal/800 kJ
10 g P · 9 g F · 11 g C

Sauces for vegetables

Egg yolk-lemon sauce

125 ml (4.5 fl oz) vegetable broth · juice of 3 lemons · grated peel of 1 untreated lemon · 100 ml (3 fl oz) basic light sauce (see p. 9) · 3 egg yolks · salt · black pepper

Bring the broth to a boil. Stir the lemon juice and lemon peel into the broth and return to the boil. Stir in the light sauce. Beat the egg yolks with a whisk and drizzle into the sauce while stirring. Thicken the sauce, remove from heat and season. **Good with cauliflower, kohlrabi, broccoli and asparagus.**

Per portion ca. 91 kcal/380 kJ
3 g P · 6 g F · 6 g C

Lentil sauce with avocado

3 tbsp olive oil · 75 g (2.5 oz) rinsed red lentils · 1 peeled and chopped avocado · 100 ml (3 fl oz) white wine · 250 ml (9 fl oz) vegetable broth · 1 tsp pesto · juice and peel of 1 untreated lemon · 3 tbsp basic tomato sauce (see p. 9) · turmeric · salt · pepper

Heat the olive oil and briefly roast the lentils and avocado in it. Pour in the wine and broth, and simmer for 15 minutes. Add the pesto and lemon juice and peel, and thicken with the basic tomato sauce. Season. **Good with black salsify.**

Per portion ca. 260 kcal/1092 kJ
6 g P · 19 g F · 13 g C

Champagne sauce

150 g (5 oz) rinsed raspberries · 200 ml (7 fl oz) vegetable broth · 2 tbsp lemon juice · 200 ml (7 fl oz) champagne · 1/2 bunch lemon balm, chopped · 3 tbsp hollandaise sauce (see p. 10) · salt · lemon pepper

Blanch 100 g (3.5 oz) raspberries in the broth, purée, then mix in the lemon juice and champagne. Reduce slightly. Add the lemon balm and thicken with the hollandaise sauce. Stir in the remaining berries and season to taste with salt and lemon pepper. **Good with green asparagus.**

Per portion ca. 80 kcal/336 kJ
2 g P · 2 g F · 5 g C

Parma sauce

3 tbsp olive oil · 2 shallots, chopped · 120 g (4 oz) Parma ham, cut into strips · 200 ml (7 fl oz) red wine · 200 ml (7 fl oz) beef broth · 1/2 bunch basil, chopped · 170 g (6 oz) blue cheese · 3 tbsp basic brown sauce (see p. 9) · salt · pepper

Sauté the shallots in the hot oil. Add the ham and continue cooking. Pour in the wine and broth and simmer for about 20 minutes. Stir in the basil and crumbled blue cheese. Thicken with brown sauce and season. **Good with savoy cabbage.**

Per portion ca. 400 kcal/1680 kJ
16 g P · 32 g F · 4 g C

Sauces for vegetables

Onion sauce

330 g (11 oz) chopped onions · 5 tbsp butter · 3 tbsp béchamel sauce (see p. 10) · 3 tbsp double cream · salt · pepper · nutmeg · lemon juice to taste

Sauté onions in butter for 10 minutes or until translucent. Heat the béchamel sauce and add to the onions. Bring to the boil and simmer 20 minutes. Purée the sauce and stir in the cream until it thickens. Season to taste with spices and lemon juice. **Good with baked vegetables.**

Per portion ca. 140 kcal/587 kJ
1 g P · 13 g F · 5 g C

Allspice sauce

500 ml (17 fl oz) chicken broth · 2 tbsp cornflour · 1/2 tsp allspice · ground nutmeg · salt · pepper · 2 tbsp lemon juice · 3 tbsp basic light sauce (see p. 9) · 1/2 bunch each parsley and coriander leaf, chopped

Bring the chicken broth to the boil, stir in the cornflour and reduce slightly. Stir in the spices and lemon juice. Thicken with the light sauce and stir in the herbs. **Good with leeks.**

Per portion ca. 623 kcal/2615 kJ
27 g P · 34 g F · 53 g C

Chilli sauce

2 tbsp cornflour · 150 ml (5 fl oz) each milk, vegetable broth · 3 jalapeño peppers, chopped · 40 g (1.5 oz) grated Emmentaler cheese · 3 tbsp basic tomato sauce (see p. 9) · 1 tbsp chopped basil · salt · pepper

Blend the flour with a bit of the milk. Heat the milk and broth and thicken with the flour paste. Add peppers, cheese and tomato sauce. Bring to the boil and mix in the basil and spices. **Good with stuffed red bell peppers.**

Per portion ca. 117 kcal/491 kJ
7 g P · 8 g F · 5 g C

Bell pepper sauce

3 yellow bell peppers ·
600 ml (1 pt 1 fl oz) vegetable broth ·
1 tsp chilli sauce · 1 crushed clove
garlic

Place the peppers under the broiler
until skin blisters, then peel and chop
the peppers. Simmer with the broth,
chilli sauce and crushed garlic for
about 20 minutes, then purée until
smooth and reheat. **Good with green
asparagus.**

Per portion ca. 53 kcal/224 kJ
2 g P · 3 g F · 4 g C

Pepper sauce

3 tbsp garlic oil · 100 g
(3.5 oz) cream of tartar · 1 tbsp green
peppercorns · 400 ml (14 fl oz) meat
broth · 1/2 bunch each thyme and
marjoram, chopped · 2 tbsp double
cream · 3 tbsp basic brown sauce (see
p. 9) · salt · pepper

Heat the oil and cream of tartar. Add
the peppercorns and broth. Reduce
slightly, then blend in the herbs and
double cream. Thicken with brown
sauce. Season. **Good with grilled
vegetables.**

Per portion ca. 110 kcal/462 kJ
7 g P · 8 g F · 2 g C

Saffron sauce

2 tbsp olive oil · 2 onions,
diced · 2 cloves garlic, chopped ·
250 g (9 oz) chopped red bell peppers
· 100 g (3.5 oz) chopped almonds ·
400 ml (14 fl oz) vegetable broth ·
1/2 tsp saffron · 3 tbsp basic light
sauce (see p. 9) · salt · Tabasco Sauce

Sauté the onions and garlic in olive
oil. Add the peppers and continue
cooking. Stir in the almonds and broth
and simmer for 20 minutes. Stir in the
saffron and light sauce. Season with
spices. **Good with spinach.**

Per portion ca. 247 kcal/1036 kJ
6 g P · 22 g F · 6 g C

Sauces for vegetables

Spinach sauce

2 tbsp olive oil · 1 onion, chopped · 2 cloves garlic, crushed · 100 g (3.5 oz) spinach cut into strips · 100 g (3.5 oz) cubed feta cheese · 400 ml (14 fl oz) vegetable broth · 2 tbsp lemon juice · 3 tbsp basic tomato sauce (see p. 9) · salt · pepper · chilli powder · 1 tsp chopped oregano

Sauté onions and garlic in the hot oil. Add and briefly sauté spinach and feta cheese. Pour in the broth and reduce the sauce somewhat. Add lemon juice and thicken with the tomato sauce. Season with spices and oregano. **Good with cucumbers, courgettes and aubergines.**

Per portion ca. 104 kcal/436 kJ
6 g P · 7 g F · 5 g C

Carrot sauce

6 tbsp olive oil · 1 tsp each turmeric, ground coriander · 350 g (12 oz) chopped carrots · 1 tbsp honey · 200 ml (7 fl oz) each vegetable broth, white wine · 2 tbsp chopped coriander leaf · 1/2 tsp chilli powder · salt · pepper · 3 tbsp lemon juice

Toast turmeric and coriander in 4 tbsp oil. Add carrots and honey and brown. Pour in broth and wine and simmer 20 minutes. Purée the sauce and bring to the boil in a pot. Stir in coriander and chilli powder. Season with spices. Stir in remaining oil and lemon juice. **Good with cauliflower and black salsify.**

Per portion ca. 239 kcal/1001 kJ
1 g P · 20 g F · 7 g C

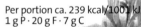

Vermouth sauce

2 tbsp butter · 50 g (2 oz) bacon cut into strips ·
1 green onion, chopped · 1 carrot, cut into small cubes ·
200 ml (7 fl oz) dry vermouth · 200 ml (7 fl oz) beef
broth · 1/2 bunch each basil and thyme, chopped ·
3 tbsp basic brown sauce (see p. 9) · salt · pepper

Render the bacon in hot butter, sauté the onions in
it, then add and briefly cook the carrots. Pour in the
vermouth and broth and simmer for 15 minutes. Stir
in the herbs and thicken with the brown sauce. **Good
with chicory and endive.**

Per portion ca. 168 kcal/705 kJ
5 g P · 8 g F · 9 g C

Yellow pea sauce

200 g (7 oz) yellow peas · 400 ml (14 fl oz)
vegetable broth · 200 ml (7 fl oz) mushroom stock ·
1/2 bunch parsley and thyme · 3 tbsp white butter sauce
(see p. 11) · salt · pepper · ground nutmeg

Rinse the peas and cook until soft in the broth and stock,
then purée. Wash, dry and chop the herbs finely. Stir into
the purée and add the white butter sauce. Season with
the spices. **Good with mushrooms and kohlrabi.**

Per portion ca. 107 kcal/448 kJ
4 g P · 6 g F · 9 g C

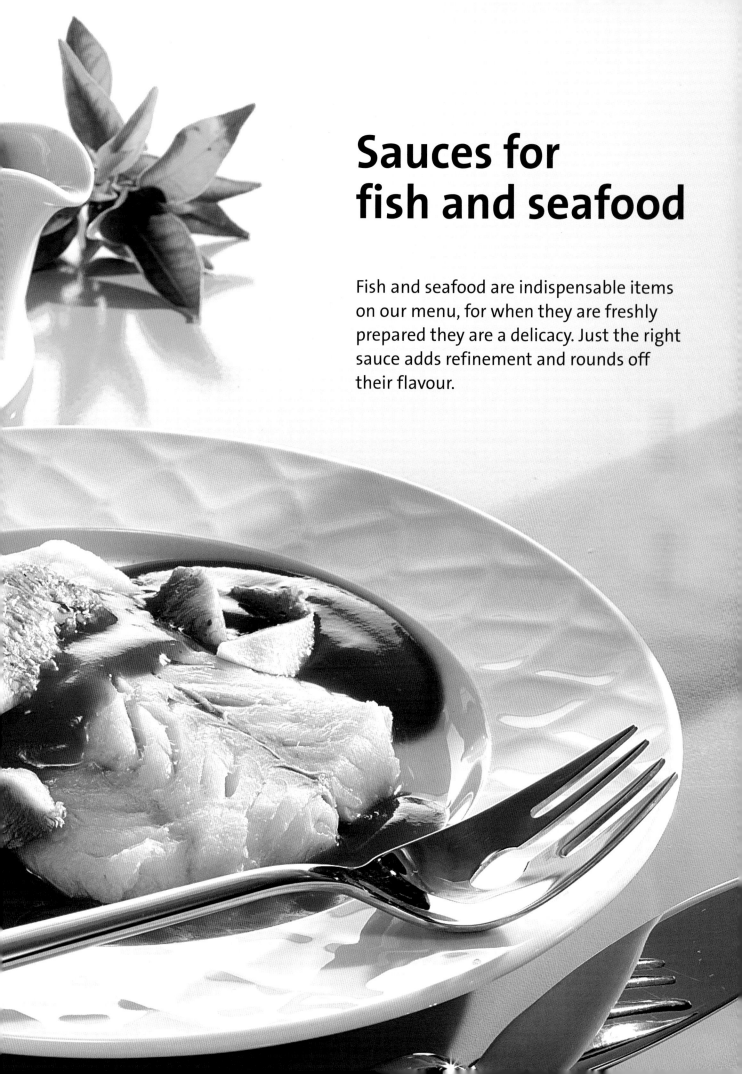

Sauces for fish and seafood

Fish and seafood are indispensable items on our menu, for when they are freshly prepared they are a delicacy. Just the right sauce adds refinement and rounds off their flavour.

Sauces for fish

Remoulade sauce

200 g (7 oz) mayonnaise
1 tbsp lemon juice
1 tsp chopped capers
1 tbsp chopped fresh herbs
1/2 tsp anchovy paste
2 finely chopped gherkins
1 finely chopped shallot
salt
pepper

1. Stir the mayonnaise with the remaining ingredients except spices until smooth.

2. Allow the sauce to draw for 10 minutes, then season with salt and pepper.

Good with roasted fish.

Per portion ca. 390 kcal/1638 kJ
1 g P · 42 g F · 3 g C

Variation 1

Prepare the remoulade sauce as in the basic recipe, but without the anchovies, capers or gherkins. Add 100 g (3.5 oz) plain yoghurt, then stir in 20 ml (scant 1 fl oz) Cognac. **Good with shellfish.**

Per portion ca. 395 kcal/1659 kJ
2 g P · 42 g F · 3 g C

Variation 2

Prepare the remoulade sauce as in the basic recipe, but without the anchovies. Add 5 tbsp ketchup and 1 tsp prepared horseradish. Season with 2 tsp white wine vinegar and a few splashes of Tabasco Sauce. **Good with shrimp and prawns.**

Per portion ca. 385 kcal/1617 kJ
1 g P · 41 g F · 4 g C

Variation 3

Prepare the remoulade sauce as in the basic recipe. Add 1/2 tsp ground saffron and 1 tsp curry powder. **Good with clams and mussels.**

Per portion ca. 393 kcal/1649 kJ
2 g P · 42 g F · 4 g C

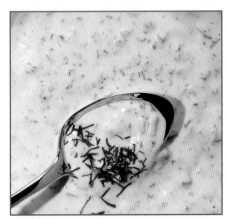

Variation 4

Prepare the remoulade sauce as in the basic recipe. Add 1 crushed clove garlic and 1 tbsp olive paste. **Good with grilled fish.**

Per portion ca. 390 kcal/1638 kJ
2 g P · 42 g F · 3 g C

Sauces for fish

Cold saffron sauce

2 egg yolks · 1/2 tsp mustard · 1 crushed clove
garlic · 1 small pack saffron · 1/2 tsp Pernod · 1/2 tsp fish
stock · 125 ml (4.5 fl oz) each olive and sunflower seed
oil · 1 tbsp tomato purée · 1 tsp each chopped basil and
tarragon · 1 tbsp crème fraîche · lemon juice · salt · pepper

Mix together the egg yolks, mustard and garlic. Stir the
saffron into the Pernod and fish stock and add this to the
egg yolk mixture. Gradually beat the oils into the sauce.
Stir in the tomato purée and the herbs and crème fraîche.
Season to taste with lemon juice and spices. **Good with
red mullet.**

Per portion ca. 610 kcal/2562 kJ
2 g P · 67 g F · 2 g C

Pernod sauce

2 tbsp butter · 150 g (5 oz) cubed kohlrabi ·
1 carrot, cut into slices · 3 green onions, sliced into rings ·
150 ml (5 fl oz) white wine · 5 tbsp Pernod · 200 ml
(7 fl oz) malt beer · 1 tbsp ground fennel seed · 1/2 bunch
chervil, chopped · sugar · 3 tbsp basic brown sauce (see
p. 9) · salt · pepper

Sauté the vegetables in the butter for 5 minutes. Pour in
the wine and Pernod, then add the malt beer. Allow the
sauce to reduce somewhat, then add the fennel seed and
chervil and season with sugar. Stir in the brown sauce and
season with salt and pepper. **Good with grilled shellfish.**

Per portion ca. 151 kcal/633 kJ
2 g P · 5 g F · 13 g C

Sorrel sauce

150 g (5 oz) sorrel · 1 tbsp butter · 100 ml (3 fl oz) white wine · 250 ml (9 fl oz) vegetable broth · 3 tbsp béchamel sauce (see p. 10) · 1 pinch sugar · salt · pepper · ground nutmeg

Wash and dry the sorrel, then blanch it briefly in salt water. Pour cold water over it and drain. Sauté in the hot butter, then purée. Pour in the wine and broth and allow to reduce somewhat. Thicken with the béchamel sauce and season with spices. **Good with grilled salmon.**

Per portion ca. 70 kcal/294 kJ
2 g P · 3 g F · 4 g C

Feta cheese sauce

2 tbsp olive oil · 1 bunch green onions, sliced in rings · 3 marinated red peppers, sliced in strips · 125 ml (4.5 fl oz) white wine · 300 g (10 oz) feta cheese · 3 tbsp basic tomato sauce (see p. 9) · salt · pepper · 1 tsp dried oregano

Heat the oil and sauté the onions and peppers for 5 minutes. Add the wine and bring to the boil. Crumble the cheese into the pan and allow it to melt. Thicken with the tomato sauce and season with the spices. **Good with grilled fish.**

Per portion ca. 275 kcal/1155 kJ
14 g P · 20 g F · 5 g C

Honey sauce

3 tbsp vegetable oil ·
1 chopped onion · 1 tbsp grated ginger · 4 tbsp lemon juice · 4 tbsp wine vinegar · 350 ml (12 fl oz) vegetable broth · flesh of 1 orange and 1 grapefruit, inner skin removed · 3 tbsp basic light sauce (see p. 9) · 1 tsp honey

Sauté the onion and ginger in the oil. Add the lemon juice, vinegar and broth and reduce for 15 minutes. Stir in the fruit flesh. Thicken with the light sauce and season with honey. **Good with salmon trout.**

Per portion ca. 166 kcal/698 kJ
1 g P · 11 g F · 13 g C

Avocado sauce

3 finely chopped shallots ·
2 tomatoes, skinned and chopped ·
1/2 red chilli, finely chopped · 1 tbsp chopped parsley · 2 peeled avocados · juice of 1 lime · 100 ml (3 fl oz) cream · salt · pepper

Purée the shallots, tomatoes, chilli, parsley and avocado flesh in a food processor. Stir in the lime juice and cream, and finally season with salt and pepper. **Good with grilled fish.**

Per portion ca. 335 kcal/1407 kJ
4 g P · 34 g F · 4 g C

Cranberry sauce

100 g (3.5 oz) jarred cranberries · 200 ml (7 fl oz) veal stock · 100 ml (3 fl oz) white wine ·
1 tbsp horseradish cream · 3 tbsp basic tomato sauce (see p. 9) · salt · pepper · sugar

Heat the cranberries in the veal stock, add the wine and horseradish and allow the sauce to reduce. Add the tomato sauce and season with salt, pepper and sugar. **Good with roasted perch.**

Per portion ca. 65 kcal/273 kJ
4 g P · 1 g F · 7 g C

Creamed parsley

2 tbsp butter · 3 chopped shallots · 200 g (7 oz) chopped parsley root · 3 bunches flat-leaf parsley, chopped · 250 ml (9 fl oz) fish stock · 150 ml (5 fl oz) white wine · 3 tbsp white butter sauce (see p. 11) · salt · pepper

Sauté the shallots and parsley root in the hot butter. Add the parsley leaf, stock and white wine and allow to reduce for a time. Thicken with the white sauce. Season. **Good with boiled fish.**

Per portion ca. 125 kcal/524 kJ
3 g P · 7 g F · 6 g C

Caraway froth

2 eggs · 2 egg yolks · 20 ml (scant 1 fl oz) caraway schnapps · 250 ml (9 fl oz) veal stock · 125 ml (4.5 fl oz) cream · salt · pepper · 1/2 tsp ground caraway seed

In a double boiler, combine the eggs, egg yolks and schnapps with 3 tbsp of the veal stock until creamy. Add the remaining stock and the cream and beat. Do not allow to boil. Season with salt, pepper and caraway seed. **Good with sole and zander.**

Per portion ca. 206 kcal/864 kJ
11 g P · 17 g F · 2 g C

Ham sauce

2 tbsp olive oil · 2 chopped onions · 100 g (3.5 oz) cubed cooked ham · 50 g (2 oz) chopped celery · 2 tomatoes in eighths · 400 ml (14 fl oz) fish stock · 1/2 bunch thyme, chopped · 3 tbsp basic brown sauce (see p. 9) · salt · pepper · nutmeg

Sauté the onions, ham and vegetables in hot oil. Add the stock and thyme and simmer for 15 minutes. Thicken with the brown sauce and season. **Good with grilled salmon.**

Per portion ca. 185 kcal/777 kJ
7 g P · 15 g F · 5 g C

Sauces for fish

Plum-ginger sauce

2 tbsp chilli oil · 100 g (3.5 oz) chopped shallots ·
3 cloves garlic, chopped · 2.5 cm (1 inch) ginger, grated ·
300 g (10 oz) fresh plums, chopped · 300 ml (10 fl oz) fish
stock · 1 tbsp dark soy sauce · 1 tsp sugar · 2 pieces star
anise · 1/2 tsp ground Szechwan pepper · salt

Heat the oil and sauté the shallots, garlic and ginger for a
few minutes. Add and briefly sauté the plums, then pour
in the stock and soy sauce and allow to reduce somewhat.
Purée the sauce. Season with the remaining ingredients.
Good with carp and trout.
Per portion ca. 92 kcal/385 kJ · 3 g P · 4 g F · 11 g C

Chervil cream sauce

1 tbsp butter · 1 bunch each chervil and parsley,
chopped · 100 ml (3 fl oz) white wine · 200 ml (7 fl oz) veal
stock · 100 ml (3 fl oz) cream · 3 tbsp béchamel sauce (see
p. 10) · salt · pepper

Heat the butter and briefly sauté the chopped herbs in it.
Pour in the wine, stock and cream and reduce somewhat.
Thicken with the béchamel sauce and season to taste
with salt and pepper. **Good with trout, salmon.**
Per portion ca. 129 kcal/543 kJ · 4 g P · 10 g F · 3 g C

Olive-tarragon sauce

3 tbsp butter · 1 chopped shallot · 150 g (5 oz) black olives with pits · 125 ml (4.5 fl oz) Noilly Prat · 250 ml (9 fl oz) fish stock · 1 cubed tomato · 1 tbsp chopped tarragon · 3 tbsp béarnaise sauce (see p. 10) · salt · pepper · lemon juice

Chop the olives. Sauté the shallot and olive pits in the hot butter, then add the Noilly Prat and fish stock. Reduce somewhat. Remove the pits from the sauce and stir in the chopped olives, tomato and tarragon. Thicken with the béarnaise sauce. Season to taste with spices and lemon juice. **Good with halibut, flounder, plaice.**

Per portion ca. 258 kcal/1082 kJ · 3 g P · 23 g F · 5 g C

Coriander-berry sauce

3 tbsp butter · 150 g (5 oz) cleaned gooseberries · 100 g (3.5 oz) yellow bell pepper, chopped · 1 clove garlic, chopped · 1 bunch coriander leaf, chopped · 100 ml (3 fl oz) white wine · 300 ml (10 fl oz) beef broth · juice and peel of 1/2 untreated lemon · 3 tbsp basic brown sauce (see p. 9) · salt · pepper

Sauté the berries and pepper in butter, then add garlic and coriander leaf. Pour in the wine and broth and reduce somewhat. Season with lemon juice and thicken with brown sauce. Season with spices. **Good with grilled dab (flounder).**

Per portion ca. 182 kcal/763 kJ · 6 g P · 12 g F · 8 g C

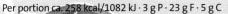

Sauces for fish

Fennel sauce

2 tbsp butter · 150 g (5 oz) cubed fennel bulb · 4 tbsp Pastis · 250 ml (9 fl oz) fish stock · 100 ml (3 fl oz) white wine · flesh and juice of 1 orange · 3 tbsp hollandaise sauce (see p. 10) · salt · pepper

Sauté the fennel in hot butter for 5 minutes. Add the Pastis, stock and white wine and cook the sauce down somewhat. Add the orange flesh and juice and finally stir in the hollandaise sauce. Season to taste. **Good with roasted zander.**

Per portion ca. 113 kcal/476 kJ
3 g P · 6 g F · 7 g C

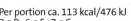

Vegetable sauce

2 peeled and cubed tomatoes · 50 g (2 oz) each chopped red and green bell peppers · 100 g (3.5 oz) peeled and minced cucumber · 1 onion, chopped · 1 clove garlic, chopped · 250 ml (9 fl oz) vegetable broth · salt · pepper · Tabasco Sauce

Purée the vegetables in a food processor. Add the broth and season to taste with salt, pepper and Tabasco Sauce. Chill the sauce in the refrigerator before serving. **Good with deep-fried sardines.**

Per portion ca. 33 kcal/140 kJ
2 g P · 1 g F · 4 g C

Barolo sauce

100 g (3.5 oz) cubed bacon · 300 g (10 oz) fresh pearl onions · 400 ml (14 fl oz) Barolo wine · 1 tsp chopped thyme · 3 tbsp basic brown sauce (see p. 9) · 2 tbsp crème fraîche · salt · pepper · lemon juice

Render the bacon and roast the pearl onions in the same pan. Add the wine and thyme and reduce the sauce. Stir in the brown sauce and crème fraîche. Season and add lemon juice to taste. **Good with grilled whiting fillet.**

Per portion ca. 308 kcal/1292 kJ
3 g P · 26 g F · 15 g C

Colourful sauce

3 tbsp clarified butter · 100 g (3.5 oz) julienned courgettes · 50 g (2 oz) cubed yellow bell pepper · 1 clove garlic, chopped · 1 tbsp tomato purée · 150 ml (5 fl oz) white wine · 250 ml (9 fl oz) vegetable broth · 1 tbsp herbes de Provence · 3 tbsp basic tomato sauce (see p. 9) · salt · pepper · ground coriander seed

Sauté vegetables in the butter, add the tomato purée, wine and broth and let sauce simmer. Stir in the herbs, thicken with tomato sauce and season with spices. **Good with roasted pike fillet.**

Per portion ca. 120 kcal/790 kJ
3 g P · 13 g F · 14 g C

Sour cream dip

200 g (7 oz) sour cream · 100 g (3.5 oz) cream · 2 onions, cut into rings · 2 apples, diced · 2 tbsp lemon juice · 1 tsp mustard powder · 1/2 tsp white pepper · 1/2 tsp ground allspice · salt · sugar · 2 tbsp chopped chives

Use a whisk to whip the sour cream with the cream until frothy. Fold in the remaining ingredients and season well. Allow to steep for a time. **Good with matjes herrings and other herring fillets.**

Per portion ca. 188 kcal/790 kJ
3 g P · 13 g F · 14 g C

Lobster sauce

3 tbsp vegetable oil · 50 g (2 oz) chopped celery · 2 tbsp green onions, chopped into rings · 200 g (7 oz) rinsed shrimp · 1 tsp lemon juice · 100 ml (3 fl oz) vermouth · 300 ml (10 fl oz) lobster stock · 3 tbsp white butter sauce (see p. 11) · salt · pepper

Cook the vegetables and shrimp in hot oil for 5 minutes. Add the lemon juice, vermouth and stock and allow the sauce to reduce slightly. Thicken with white butter sauce and season. **Good with bream.**

Per portion ca. 157 kcal/660 kJ
11 g P · 6 g F · 2 g C

Sauces for fish

Horseradish sauce

250 ml (9 fl oz) veal stock · 250 ml (9 fl oz) milk · 100 g (3.5 oz) freshly ground horseradish · 50 g (2 oz) ground almonds · 1 tbsp lemon juice · 5 tbsp crème fraîche · 3 tbsp béchamel sauce (see p. 10) · cayenne

Bring the stock and milk to a boil, add horseradish and almonds and allow the sauce to reduce somewhat. Add lemon juice and crème fraîche and thicken with the béchamel sauce. Season with cayenne. **Good with poached monkfish.**

Per portion ca. 183 kcal/770 kJ
10 g P · 12 g F · 8 g C

Trianon sauce

1 tbsp olive oil · 5 chopped shallots · 4 tbsp white wine · 2–3 tbsp mayonnaise · 1 tbsp tomato purée · 3 finely chopped peppercorn pickles · 1/2 red bell pepper, chopped · salt · pepper · sugar

Heat the oil and sauté shallots. Add the wine and simmer 10 minutes, then purée. Mix the cooled purée, mayonnaise and tomato purée and stir in the pickles and pepper. Season to taste. **Good with grilled mackerel.**

Per portion ca. 167 kcal/700 kJ
1 g P · 15 g F · 5 g C

Beetroot cream

3 tbsp olive oil · 2 chopped shallots · 250 g (9 oz) beetroot, cut into strips · 125 ml (4.5 fl oz) white wine · 400 ml (14 fl oz) fish stock · 1/2 bunch parsley, chopped · 3 tbsp red butter sauce (see p. 11) · salt · pepper

Heat the oil and braise the shallots and beetroot in it. Add the white wine and stock and reduce somewhat. Stir in the parsley, add the red butter sauce and season. **Good with roasted sole.**

Per portion ca. 173 kcal/726 kJ
4 g P · 12 g F · 9 g C

Dill sauce

3 tbsp butter · 1 chopped onion · 200 ml (7 fl oz) fish stock · 100 ml (3 fl oz) white wine · 100 g (3.5 oz) cream · 1 bunch dill, chopped · 3 tbsp basic light sauce (see p. 9) · salt · pepper · nutmeg · wine vinegar

Sauté the onion in the hot butter. Pour in the stock, wine and cream and simmer for 10 minutes. Stir in the dill. Blend in the light sauce and season to taste with the spices and vinegar. **Good with plaice and codfish.**

Per portion ca. 174 kcal/730 kJ
2 g P · 15 g F · 4 g C

Fig sauce

40 ml (1.5 fl oz) tomato juice · 150 g (5 oz) peeled, chopped figs · 1 tin tomatoes (250 g/9 oz) · 4 tbsp lemon juice · grated ginger · cinnamon · 10 ml (.5 fl oz) Madeira · 3 tbsp basic tomato sauce (see p. 9) · 2 figs, cut into slices

Heat the tomato juice and simmer the figs and tomatoes in it. Purée the sauce. Flavour the sauce with the lemon juice, ginger, cinnamon and Madeira. Thicken with the tomato sauce. Stir in the fig slices. **Good with halibut.**

Per portion ca. 107 kcal/450 kJ
3 g P · 2 g F · 18 g C

Apricot-pepper sauce

2 tbsp butter · 200 g (7 oz) tinned apricot slices, drained · 3 tsp red peppercorns · 3 tbsp brandy · 350 ml (12 fl oz) apricot juice · 6 tbsp cream · 3 tbsp basic light sauce (see p. 9) · salt · pepper · Tabasco Sauce

Sauté the apricot slices in the hot butter for 5 minutes. Add the peppercorns, brandy and apricot juice and reduce somewhat. Stir in the cream and thicken with the light sauce. Season. **Good with steamed jumbo shrimps.**

Per portion ca. 177 kcal/742 kJ
2 g P · 9 g F · 19 g C

Sauces for fish

Raisin cream sauce

2 tbsp butter · 2 chopped onions · 250 ml (9 fl oz) white wine · 225 g (8 oz) cream · 150 g (5 oz) crème fraîche · 1 bunch dill, chopped · 150 g (5 oz) raisins, soaked in water · 3 tbsp basic light sauce (see p. 9) · salt · pepper · lemon juice

Sauté the onions in hot butter. Add the wine and cream and reduce. Stir in the crème fraîche, dill and raisins, thicken with the light sauce and season. **Good with trout.**

Per portion ca. 463 kcal/1943 kJ
4 g P · 31 g F · 32 g C

Thai curry sauce

2 tbsp sunflower oil · 100 g (3.5 oz) snow peas · 100 g (3.5 oz) chopped mushrooms · 100 g (3.5 oz) cucumber, julienned · 1 onion, chopped · 2 tomatoes, diced · 200 ml (7 fl oz) each vegetable broth and fish stock · 1 bunch coriander leaf, chopped · 2 tbsp chopped lemon grass · 3 tbsp basic tomato sauce (see p. 9) · salt · pepper · 2 tsp red curry paste

Heat the oil and sauté vegetables. Add broth and stock and bring to the boil, then add coriander and lemon grass and reduce for 10 minutes. Thicken with tomato sauce and season with spices. **Good with ocean perch or redfish.**

Per portion ca. 112 kcal/468 kJ · 6 g P · 7 g F · 8 g C

Vodka-caviar sauce

400 ml (14 fl oz) vegetable broth · 1 avocado, peeled and cubed · 20 g (1 oz) black caviar · 20 g (scant 1 oz) red caviar · 4 tbsp vodka · 3 tbsp lemon juice · 1 tsp horseradish cream · 3 tbsp basic light sauce (see p. 9) · salt · pepper · Tabasco Sauce

Simmer the avocado in the broth, then purée. Add the caviar, vodka and lemon juice to the purée, then stir in the horseradish. Thicken with the light sauce and season with salt, pepper and Tabasco. **Good with crab, lobster and langoustine.**

Per portion ca. 183 kcal/767 kJ · 4 g P · 17 g F · 3 g C

Grapes and wine sauce

2 tbsp butter · 1 shallot, chopped · 200 ml (7 fl oz) pinot noir · 200 ml (7 fl oz) fish stock · 200 g (7 oz) washed and seeded blue grapes · 3 tbsp basic light sauce (see p. 9) · salt · pepper

Melt the butter in a fry pan and sauté the shallots. Pour in the pinot noir and fish stock and reduce somewhat. Stir in the grapes. Thicken with the basic light sauce and season with salt and pepper. **Good with sole.**

Per portion ca. 117 kcal/492 kJ
1 g P · 5 g F · 10 g C

Sauces for fish

Bean sauce

2 garlic cloves, chopped · 1
cm (1/2 in) fresh ginger, grated ·
1 chopped green chilli pepper · 4 tbsp
peanut oil · 3 tbsp softened and
chopped black beans · 1 tsp cornflour ·
350 ml (12 fl oz) veal stock · 1 tbsp
soy sauce · 2 tbsp sherry

Sauté the garlic, ginger and chilli in the
hot oil for 2 minutes. Add the black
beans and continue sautéing. Stir the
cornflour into some of the stock and
add to the beans along with the
remaining ingredients . **Good with
clams, mussels and seafood.**

Per portion ca. 89 kcal/373 kJ
7 g P · 6 g F · 2 g C

Cardinal sauce

250 ml (9 fl oz) fish stock ·
250 ml (9 fl oz) mushroom stock ·
500 ml (17 fl oz) béchamel sauce (see
p. 10) · 75 g (2.5 oz) cooked lobster
meat · 50 g (2 oz) butter · chopped
red bell pepper · cayenne pepper

Bring the fish and mushroom stock
to a boil and reduce by half. Add the
béchamel sauce, heat and then strain.
Purée the lobster meat, mix with the
butter and red bell pepper and stir
into the sauce. Season to taste. **Good
with ocean fish.**

Per portion ca. 255 kcal/1071 kJ
9 g P · 20 g F · 10 g C

Berry dip

400 g (14 oz) cranberry
preserves (from a jar) · 100 g (3.5 oz)
crème fraîche · a pinch cinnamon ·
20 ml (scant 1 fl oz) rum

Mix all the ingredients together and
purée to the desired consistency.
Good with red mullet and whitefish.

Per portion ca. 348 kcal/1460 kJ
1 g P · 8 g F · 67 g C

Date sauce

2 tbsp butter · 1 chopped onion · 150 g (5 oz) fresh dates, chopped · 100 g (3.5 oz) dessicated coconut · 400 ml (14 fl oz) lobster stock · 1/2 bunch lemon balm, chopped · 1 tbsp double cream · 3 tbsp light soy sauce · 3 tbsp basic brown sauce (see p. 9) · salt · pepper

Heat butter and sauté the onion, dates and coconut. Pour in the stock and reduce slightly. Stir in remaining ingredients and thicken with the brown sauce. Season. **Good with langoustine.**

Per portion ca. 348 kcal/1460 kJ
5 g P · 23 g F · 29 g C

Dandelion dip

3 tbsp butter · 1 chopped onion · 2 cloves garlic, chopped · 1 bunch baby dandelion, chopped · 400 ml (14 fl oz) vegetable broth · 3 tbsp honey · 100 g (3.5 oz) asparagus pieces (tinned or jarred) · 3 tbsp basic light sauce (see p. 9)

Heat butter and sauté the onion, garlic and dandelion for 5 minutes, then purée. Pour in the broth and reduce somewhat. Stir in the honey and asparagus and thicken with the light sauce. **Good with crayfish.**

Per portion ca. 88 kcal/370 kJ
1 g P · 6 g F · 9 g C

Bay leaf sauce

3 tbsp sunflower seed oil · 1 clove garlic, chopped · 200 g (7 oz) cubed potatoes · 1 tsp ground bay leaf · 400 ml (14 fl oz) fish stock · 1 tbsp chopped tarragon · 3 tbsp basic tomato sauce (see p. 9) · salt · pepper

Heat the oil and sauté the garlic and potatoes for 5 minutes. Add the bay leaf and stock, simmer for 5 minutes, then purée the sauce. Stir in the tarragon and tomato sauce. Season to taste. **Good with mullet.**

Per portion ca. 150 kcal/628 kJ
3 g P · 11 g F · 9 g C

Sauces for fish

Prince sauce

200 ml (7 fl oz) veal stock · 125 ml (4.5 fl oz) white wine · 1/2 bunch mixed herbs, chopped · 1 chopped onion · 6 white peppercorns · 25 g (1 oz) truffles (tinned) · 100 g (3.5 oz) crabmeat (tinned) · 3 tbsp white butter sauce (see p. 11) · salt · pepper · cayenne pepper

Heat the stock and wine and bring to the boil with herbs, onion and crushed peppercorns. Reduce somewhat. Cut the truffles into strips, remove all shell from the crabmeat and stir into the sauce. Thicken with the butter sauce and season to taste. **Good with zander, angler fish, salmon.**

Per portion ca. 99 kcal/414 kJ · 9 g P · 3 g F · 4 g C

Spicy peanut sauce

2 tbsp peanut butter · 200 ml (7 fl oz) milk · 200 ml (7 fl oz) vegetable broth · 4 tbsp soy sauce · 1 pinch sambal oelek · 2 cloves garlic, crushed · 2 tbsp chopped coriander · 3 tbsp basic brown sauce (see p. 9) · salt · pepper · sugar

Combine the peanut butter and the milk and heat the mix, along with the vegetable broth. Stir in the soy sauce and sambal oelek. Allow to reduce for about 10 minutes. Add the garlic and coriander and thicken with the brown sauce. Season. **Good with grilled swordfish.**

Per portion ca. 77 kcal/324 kJ · 3 g P · 5 g F · 5 g C

Garlic-sunflower seed dip

2 slices white bread · 250 ml (9 fl oz) milk · 100 g (3.5 oz) sunflower seeds · 2 cloves garlic · 125 g (4.5 oz) cream · 1/2 bunch flat-leaf parsley, chopped · salt · white pepper · lemon juice

Remove the crusts from the bread and soak in the milk. Purée in a food processor with the sunflower seeds and crushed garlic. Stir in the cream and then the parsley. Allow to draw for a time, then season with salt, pepper and lemon juice. **Good with grilled sardines and mackerel.**

Per portion ca. 295 kcal/1239 kJ · 9 g P · 24 g F · 11 g C

Wasabi-horseradish sauce

100 ml (3 fl oz) lobster stock · 50 ml (2 fl oz) soy sauce · 200 ml (7 fl oz) orange juice · 1 chopped onion · 100 g (3.5 oz) horseradish, sliced into thin strips · 1 tsp wasabi · 1 clove garlic · 1 tbsp sugar · 1 tsp chopped marinated ginger · 3 tbsp basic tomato sauce (see p. 9) · salt · pepper

Heat up the stock, soy sauce and orange juice. Stir in the onion, horseradish and wasabi, then crush the garlic in, add the sugar and let the sauce reduce somewhat. Stir in the ginger and add the tomato sauce. Season. **Good with steamed fish and seafood.**

Per portion ca. 76 kcal/317 kJ · 3 g P · 1 g F · 12 g C

Sauces for fish

Chantilly sauce

1 tbsp butter · 1/2 bunch green onions, chopped · 300 ml (10 fl oz) hollandaise sauce (see p. 10) · 100 ml (3 fl oz) whipped cream · 1 bunch chives, chopped

Sauté the green onions in hot butter, stir in the hollandaise sauce and heat through. Gently fold in the whipped cream and chives. **Good with lobster and crab.**

Per portion ca. 168 kcal/704 kJ
5 g P · 14 g F · 5 g C

Anise sauce

2 tbsp butter · 1 chopped mango · 125 ml (4.5 fl oz) mango juice · juice of 1 grapefruit · 1/2 tsp ground anise seed · 1/2 tsp ground coriander seed · 1/2 tsp turmeric · 150 g (5 oz) sour cream · 3 tbsp basic light sauce (see p. 9) · salt

Sauté the mango in the hot butter for 1 minute, than add the juices and spices and reduce the sauce some. Stir in the sour cream and thicken with the light sauce. Add salt to taste. **Good with turbot.**

Per portion ca. 135 kcal/568 kJ
2 g P · 9 g F · 11 g C

Five-spice sauce

2 tbsp butter · 1/2 bunch each green onions and lemon grass, finely chopped · 300 ml (10 fl oz) fish stock · 100 ml (3 fl oz) white wine · 125 g (4.5 oz) double cream · soy sauce · five spice powder

Sauté the green onions and lemon grass in hot butter. Pour in the stock and wine and allow to reduce somewhat. Stir in the cream and season with soy sauce and five spice powder. **Good with salmon.**

Per portion ca. 167 kcal/700 kJ
2 g P · 15 g F · 3 g C

Sprouts sauce

100 g (3.5 oz) fresh radish sprouts · 250 ml (9 fl oz) white wine · 250 ml (9 fl oz) fish stock · 250 ml (9 fl oz) cream · 3 tbsp white butter sauce (see p. 11) · salt · pepper

Wash sprouts and purée 80 g (slightly less than 3 oz) of them. Bring the wine, stock and cream to the boil and reduce by half. Add the sprouts purée to this, then pour in the butter sauce and season. Stir in the remaining sprouts. **Good with trout.**

Per portion ca. 340 kcal/1428 kJ
3 g P · 30 g F · 5 g C

Fruity sauce

2 tbsp sunflower seed oil · 2 onions, chopped · 2 cloves garlic, crushed · 300 ml (10 fl oz) passion fruit juice · 250 ml (9 fl oz) vegetable broth · 250 g (9 oz) julienned carrots · 150 g (5 oz) frozen peas · flesh of 1 orange with no skin · 3 tbsp basic brown sauce (see p. 9) · salt · pepper

Heat the oil and sauté the onion and garlic. Pour in the juice and broth and simmer 5 minutes. Stir in the vegetables and orange. Thicken with brown sauce and season. **Good with ling.**

Per portion ca. 213 kcal/896 kJ
7 g P · 9 g F · 23 g C

Mustard sauce

1 tbsp butter · 2 chopped shallots · 350 ml (12 fl oz) veal stock · 100 g (3.5 oz) cream · 3 tbsp Dijon mustard · 2 tsp chopped capers · 3 tbsp white butter sauce (see p. 11) · salt · white pepper

Sauté the shallots in the heated butter. Pour in the veal stock and cream and allow to reduce somewhat. Stir in the mustard and capers. Thicken with the butter sauce and season to taste. **Good with boiled fish.**

Per portion ca. 202 kcal/847 kJ
8 g P · 17 g F · 4 g C

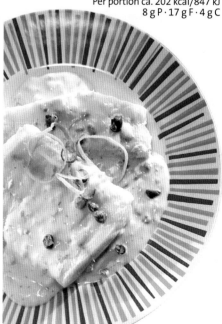

Sauces for game, poultry and meat

Fruit sauces, sauces flavoured with liqueur or wine, and sauces made aromatic with herbs all elicit fine flavours from game, poultry and meat.

Sauces for meat

Cold horse-radish sauce

50 g (2 oz) fresh horseradish

125 ml (4.5 fl oz) white wine vinegar

2 tbsp beef broth

1 pinch salt

1 pinch sugar

1. Peel the horseradish and grate finely. Place in a bowl.

2. Pour the wine vinegar and then the broth onto the horseradish and let stand 2 minutes. Purée with a handheld blender until smooth and season to taste with salt and sugar.

Good with cooked beef and pork.

Per portion ca. 253 kcal/1061 kJ
17 g P · 14 g F · 13 g C

Variation 1

Prepare the horseradish sauce as in the basic recipe, and mix in 300 g (10 oz) peeled and grated apple. Instead of a pinch of sugar, stir in 30 g (1 oz) sugar (or to taste). Serve immediately. **Good with pork shoulder.**

Per portion ca. 323 kcal/1355 kJ
18 g P · 15 g F · 29 g C

Variation 2

Prepare the horseradish sauce as in the basic recipe. Stir 300 g (10 oz) peeled and grated apple into 4 tbsp orange juice and 2 tbsp lemon juice and add this mixture to the horseradish. Add aroma with a bit of grated orange peel. **Good with roast game.**

Per portion ca. 298 kcal/1250 kJ
18 g P · 15 g F · 23 g C

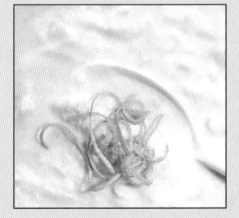

Variation 3

Prepare the horseradish sauce as in the basic recipe, but instead of the vinegar use 250 ml (9 fl oz) cream. Substitute sweet paprika for the sugar. Serve immediately. **Good with roast ham.**

Per portion ca. 428 kcal/1800 kJ
19 g P · 33 g F · 13 g C

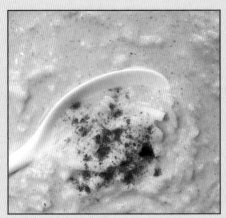

Variation 4

Prepare the horseradish sauce as in the basic recipe, but leave out the vinegar. Fold in 200 ml (7 fl oz) firmly whipped cream and 50 g (2 oz) ground almonds. **Good with grilled meat.**

Per portion ca. 465 kcal/1953 kJ
21 g P · 36 g F · 14 g C

Sauces for meat

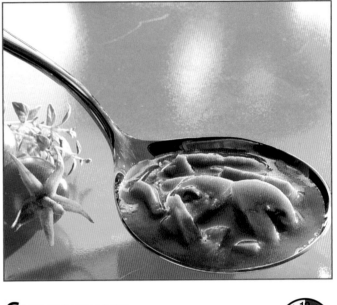

Green peppercorn sauce

1 tbsp safflower oil · 1 finely chopped onion ·
20 ml (scant 1 fl oz) white wine · 100 ml (3 fl oz) beef
broth · 3 tbsp Calvados · 125 ml (4.5 fl oz) cream · 2 tsp
green peppercorns · 3 tbsp basic light sauce (see p. 9) ·
salt · pepper

Sauté the onion in the hot oil. Pour in the white wine,
broth and Calvados and allow to reduce somewhat. Add
the cream. Stir in the peppercorns and add the light sauce.
Season with salt and pepper. **Good with pork chops.**

Per portion ca. 157 kcal/660 kJ · 3 g P · 12 g F · 4 g C

Gypsy sauce

20 g (scant 1 oz) butter · 10 g (1 oz) flour · 375 ml
(13 fl oz) beef stock · 2 slices cooked ham, cut into strips ·
5 mushrooms, sliced · 2 tbsp Madeira · salt · cayenne ·
3 tbsp basic tomato sauce (see p. 9)

Melt the butter and make a roux with the flour. Pour in
the broth and bring to the boil while stirring. Simmer
10 minutes, then add the ham and mushrooms. Season
with the Madeira and spices, then add the tomato sauce.
Good with veal cutlet.

Per portion ca. 139 kcal/583 kJ · 10 g P · 9 g · 5

Walnut-fig sauce

1 tbsp olive oil · 30 g (1 oz) chopped walnuts ·
100 ml (3 fl oz) lamb stock · 175 ml (6 fl oz) apple juice ·
8 dried figs, chopped · 1/2 tsp salt · 3 tbsp basic light
sauce (see p. 9)

Toast the nuts in hot oil, then pour in the stock and juice.
Reduce somewhat, then add the figs and season. Thicken
with the light sauce. **Good with lamb cutlets.**

Per portion ca. 265 kcal/1113 kJ · 6 g P · 11 g F · 36 g C

Balsamic fruit sauce

1 tbsp sunflower seed oil · 2 chopped shallots ·
250 ml (9 fl oz) veal stock · 8 dried plums, chopped ·
1/4 tsp black pepper · 1 tbsp balsamic vinegar · 1 tsp
grated peel from an untreated lemon · 1/2 tsp sugar ·
1 tbsp basic brown sauce (see p. 9)

Sauté the shallots in the heated oil. Add 100 ml (3 fl oz) of
the veal stock and simmer for 3 minutes. Add the plums
and remaining stock, along with the pepper. Simmer for
5 minutes longer, then stir in the remaining ingredients.
Good with fillet steak.

Per portion ca. 193 kcal/810 kJ · 7 g P · 4 g F · 30 g C

Sauces for meat

Spring sauce

2 tbsp butter · 2 cloves garlic, chopped · 1 bunch green onions, chopped · 1/2 bunch basil, chopped · 200 ml (7 fl oz) white wine · 200 ml (7 fl oz) poultry stock · 2 tbsp mustard · 50 g (2 oz) grated parmesan cheese · 3 tbsp basic light sauce (see p. 9) · salt · pepper

Heat the butter and sauté the garlic and onions. Add the basil, wine and stock and reduce. Stir in the mustard, cheese and light sauce, thicken and season. **Good with poached poultry breast.**

Per portion ca. 189 kcal/795 kJ
8 g P · 12 g F · 4 g C

Green pepper sauce

2 tbsp butter · 1 chopped onion · 1 chopped clove garlic · 1 chopped green bell pepper · 300 ml (10 fl oz) vegetable broth · 100 ml (3 fl oz) cream · 2 tbsp Armagnac · 3 tbsp basic light sauce (see p. 9) · salt · pepper · cayenne · 1 tsp sugar

Heat the butter and sauté the onion and garlic in it. Add the pepper and continue cooking. Pour in the broth and cream and simmer. Purée the sauce, add the Armagnac and stir in the light sauce. Season. **Good with grilled meat.**

Per portion ca. 146 kcal/614 kJ
2 g P · 14 g F · 4 g C

Cumberland sauce

Chopped peel and juice of 1 orange · 1 chopped shallot · 4 tbsp red wine · 150 g (5 oz) red currant jelly · 2 tbsp port wine · 1 tsp Cognac · 1 pinch ground ginger · 1/4 tsp mustard powder · cayenne

Cook the orange peel and shallot in the wine until almost jelled. Mix together the red currant jelly with the port, Cognac and 3 tbsp orange juice. Season and blend with the red wine farce. **Good with meat pâtés.**

Per portion ca. 143 kcal/600 kJ
1 g P · 1 g F · 31 g C

Adlon sauce

2 egg yolks · 1 tbsp butter · 1 tbsp lemon juice · salt · pepper · 100 ml (3 fl oz) vegetable broth · 1 tbsp anchovy paste · 1 tsp soy sauce · 1/2 tsp mustard · 1 tsp caviar

Blend together the egg yolks, butter, lemon juice, salt and pepper. Stir until creamy over warm but not boiling water in a double boiler. Add the broth, then let cool. Stir in the remaining ingredients and cool in the refrigerator. **Good with boiled or grilled cold meat.**

Per portion ca. 75 kcal/316 kJ
3 g P · 7 g F · 1 g C

Gooseberry sauce

250 g (9 oz) cleaned gooseberries · 250 ml (9 fl oz) white wine · 1 pinch sugar · 2 tbsp béchamel sauce (see p. 10) · 1 egg yolk · 2 tbsp cream · 1 tbsp lemon juice

Blanch the gooseberries for 3 minutes. Bring the white wine to a boil with the sugar, add the berries and simmer for 15 minutes. Purée the sauce and then add the béchamel sauce. Whisk the egg yolk with the cream and add these to the sauce. Season with lemon. **Good with duck and goose.**

Per portion ca. 108 kcal/453 kJ
2 g P · 3 g F · 9 g C

Sangrita sauce

2 tbsp butter · 1 chopped onion · 400 ml (14 fl oz) sangrita · 1/2 bunch sage, chopped · 2 tbsp black currant jelly · 1 tbsp crème fraîche · 3 tbsp basic brown sauce (see p. 9) · salt · pepper

Sauté the onion in the heated butter, pour in the sangrita and reduce somewhat. Add the sage and simmer for 5 minutes. Stir in the jelly and crème fraîche, thicken with the brown sauce and season. **Good with venison medallions.**

Per portion ca. 155 kcal/650 kJ
1 g P · 6 g F · 8 g C

Sauces for meat

Wine-mustard sauce

2 tbsp butter · 1 chopped onion · 1 bunch chervil, chopped · 1/2 bunch flat-leaf parsley, chopped · 200 ml (7 fl oz) each white wine, vegetable broth · 5 chopped peppercorns · 2 tbsp lime juice · 2 tbsp sweet mustard · 1 tsp curry powder · 3 tbsp basic light sauce (see p. 9) · salt · pepper

Sauté the onion and herbs in the heated butter, add the wine and broth and simmer for 10 minutes. Stir in the peppercorns, lime juice, mustard and curry powder and thicken with the light sauce. Season. **Good with pâtés.**

Per portion ca. 116 kcal/485 kJ
1 g P · 6 g F · 6 g C

Tomato-vegetable sauce

3 tbsp oil · 50 g (2 oz) broccoli flowerets · 1 chopped tomato · 1 carrot, cut into slivers · 50 g (2 oz) green beans · 2 dried red chillies · 400 ml (14 fl oz) veal stock · 1 tsp cumin · 1/4 tsp turmeric · 2 cloves garlic, crushed · 3 tbsp basic tomato sauce (see p. 9) · salt · pepper

Sauté the vegetables in hot oil, crumble in the chillies and pour in the stock. Allow the sauce to reduce a bit, then stir in the cumin, turmeric and garlic. Thicken with the basic tomato sauce and season. **Good with braised beef.**

Per portion ca. 149 kcal/625 kJ
9 g P · 10 g F · 5 g C

Pastis-mustard sauce

200 ml (7 fl oz) beef stock · 150 ml (5 fl oz) sauer-kraut juice · 2 cloves · 1 bay leaf · 2 red onions, sliced · 2 leek stems, cut in rings · 4 tbsp sherry · 1/2 bunch tarragon, chopped · 3 tbsp Dijon mustard · salt · pepper · paprika · 3 tbsp basic light sauce (see p. 9) · 2 tbsp Pastis

Bring the beef stock, sauerkraut juice, cloves and bay leaf to a boil and reduce for 15 minutes. Add the onion and leeks and simmer 5 minutes. Add the sherry, tarragon, mustard and spices. Strain the sauce, then thicken with the light sauce. Stir in the Pastis. **Good with roast beef.**

Per portion ca. 95 kcal/400 kJ
7 g P · 3 g F · 8 g C

Rosemary-mustard sauce

1 tbsp clarified butter · 250 g (9 oz) shallots in strips · 150 g (5 oz) halved baby carrots · 400 ml (14 fl oz) beef stock · 2 tbsp hot mustard · 1 tbsp chopped rosemary · 3 tbsp basic brown sauce · salt · pepper · 1/2 tsp sugar

Sauté the shallots in the heated butter, add the carrots and sauté briefly. Pour in the beef stock and reduce somewhat. Stir in the mustard and rosemary, then thicken with the brown sauce. Season with salt, pepper and sugar. **Good with beef shin and leg.**

Per portion ca. 106 kcal/445 kJ
8 g P · 6 g F · 5 g C

Sauces for meat

Mango-mustard sauce

2 small mangoes · 125 ml (4.5 fl oz) white wine · 3 tbsp sweet mustard · 1–2 tbsp basic white sauce (see p. 9) · salt · black pepper · 1 pinch cayenne

Peel and chop the mangoes and cook in the wine for 10 minutes. Let cool, then purée. Stir in the mustard and season with the basic white sauce. Season to taste. **Good with cold roasts, poultry.**

Per portion ca. 79 kcal/330 kJ
1 g P · 1 g F · 11 g C

Cassis sauce

2 tbsp balsamic vinegar · 4 tbsp cassis liqueur · 100 ml (3 fl oz) each beef broth, poultry stock · 3 tbsp crème fraîche · 1 tbsp black currant jelly · 1/2 tsp Dijon mustard · salt · white pepper

Bring the vinegar and cassis to a boil, add the broth and stock and reduce until syrupy. Stir in the crème fraîche and jelly and season with mustard, salt and pepper. **Good with duck breast and maize-fed chicken.**

Per portion ca. 77 kcal/321 kJ
3 g P · 4 g F · 4 g C

Truffle sauce

2 tbsp butter · 40 g (1.5 oz) black truffles · 4 tbsp red port · 100 ml (3 fl oz) each red wine, meat broth · 3 tbsp basic brown sauce (see p. 9) · salt · pepper · 1 tbsp chilled butter

Clean the truffles and cut into thin strips. Sauté briefly in the butter, then pour in the port, red wine and broth and allow to reduce somewhat. Thicken with the brown sauce and season. Stir in the chilled butter. **Good with guinea fowl.**

Per portion ca. 114 kcal/477 kJ
3 g P · 8 g F · 3 g C

Apple sauce

500 g (17 oz) cooking apples, peeled and chopped · 3 tbsp honey · 2 tsp white wine · 3 cloves · 1 cinnamon stick · grated lemon peel · 3 tsp butter · 3 tbsp sour cream

Combine apples, honey, wine, spices and lemon peel in a saucepan and let simmer for about 15 minutes. Remove the cloves and cinnamon stick and purée the sauce. Heat again and stir in the butter and sour cream. **Good with roast pork.**

Per portion ca. 158 kcal/662 kJ
1 g P · 7 g F · 21 g C

Sour cherry sauce

1 tbsp sugar · peel of 1/2 orange, cut into strips · 200 g (7 oz) sour cherries (from a jar) · 200 ml (7 fl oz) game stock · 1 tbsp white butter sauce (see p. 11) · 100 ml (3 fl oz) cream · 1 tbsp Kirsch · salt · cayenne

Caramelise the sugar, then stir in peel and cherries. Add the stock and reduce somewhat. Stir in the butter sauce and cream and simmer for 5 minutes. Season with Kirsch and spices. **Good with game and pheasant.**

Per portion ca. 167 kcal/702 kJ
5 g P · 12 g F · 10 g C

Mint sauce

2 chopped shallots · 1 tbsp butter · 20 chopped peppermint leaves · 10 crushed peppercorns · 4 tbsp white wine · 3 tbsp white balsamic vinegar · 3 tbsp béarnaise sauce (see p. 10) · salt · pepper

Sauté the shallots in the butter, then add peppermint leaves and peppercorns. Pour in the wine and vinegar. Reduce the sauce to one third. Strain the sauce, then stir in the béarnaise sauce and season. **Good with lamb.**

Per portion ca. 81 kcal/338 kJ
1 g P · 7 g F · 2 g C

Sauces for meat

Olive and garlic sauce

4 tbsp olive oil · 60 g (2 oz) flour · 500 ml (17 fl oz) chicken broth · 1 skinned and finely diced red bell pepper · 75 g (2.5 oz) chopped green olives · 1 crushed clove garlic · salt · black pepper · 2 tbsp chopped chives

Heat 3 tbsp of the oil and add the flour, making a roux. Stir in the broth and bring to the boil. Ladle off any foam and stir in the pepper. Simmer 20 minutes. Stir in olives and garlic and simmer another 2 minutes. Add the remaining oil, spices and chives. **Good with roast chicken.**

Per portion ca. 241 kcal/1012 kJ · 8 g P · 22 g F · 3 g C

Chervil-mushroom sauce

50 g (2 oz) butter · 100 g (3.5 oz) chopped horse mushrooms · 15 g (1 oz) porcini mushrooms soaked (in 60 ml/2 fl oz water), diced · 300 ml (10 fl oz) béchamel sauce (see p. 10) · 1 tbsp each soy sauce, lemon juice · 1/4 tsp grated lemon peel · salt · black pepper · 2 tbsp chopped chervil

Sauté mushrooms in butter until soft, then add porcini mushrooms and sauté 2 minutes more. Sieve the porcini soaking water into this sauce, then stir in béchamel and soy sauces. Simmer 20 minutes. Season with remaining ingredients. **Good with pheasant.**

Per portion ca. 173 kcal/725 kJ · 3 g P · 15 g F · 6 g C

Nut-sambal sauce

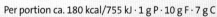

2 tbsp oil · 2 chopped shallots · 1 clove garlic,
chopped · 1 tsp grated ginger · 1 tsp ground mace · 1/2 tsp
turmeric · 1 tsp lemon juice · 400 ml (14 fl oz) poultry stock ·
2 tbsp chopped cashew nuts · 1/2 tsp sambal oelek ·
3 tbsp basic tomato sauce (see p. 9) · salt · pepper

Heat oil and sauté the shallots and garlic. Mix in spices,
then stir in the lemon juice. Pour in the stock and reduce
some. Stir in the nuts and sambal oelek, then thicken with
tomato sauce. Season. **Good with roast turkey breast.**

Per portion ca. 165 kcal/693 kJ · 7 g P · 13 g F · 5 g C

Pineapple-rum sauce

3 tbsp oil · 1 bunch green onions, chopped ·
1 dried chilli · 1 chopped baby pineapple · 300 ml (10 fl oz)
pineapple juice · 100 ml (3 fl oz) rum · 1 tsp brown sugar ·
Tabasco Sauce · salt · pepper · 3 tbsp basic brown sauce
(see p. 9)

Sauté the green onions in the oil and add the dried chilli.
Add the pineapple pieces and briefly sauté. Pour in the
juice and rum and simmer for 10 minutes. Season with
brown sugar, Tabasco Sauce, salt and pepper. Thicken with
the brown sauce. **Good with roasted guinea fowl.**

Per portion ca. 180 kcal/755 kJ · 1 g P · 10 g F · 7 g C

Sauces for meat

Sorrel-wine sauce

2 tbsp butter · 2 shallots, chopped · 1 clove garlic, crushed · 1 bunch sorrel, chopped · 1 tomato, peeled and chopped · 4 tbsp dry vermouth · 100 ml (3 fl oz) white wine · 100 ml (3 fl oz) vegetable broth · 4 tbsp sour cream · salt · cayenne · curry powder · 1 tbsp lemon juice

Heat butter and sauté the shallots and garlic. Add the sorrel and tomato. Pour in the vermouth, wine and broth and reduce somewhat. Purée the sauce, stir in the sour cream and season. **Good with turkey.**

Per portion ca. 113 kcal/475 kJ
2 g P · 8 g F · 4 g C

Madeira sauce

2 tbsp olive oil · 60 g (2 oz) bacon, cut into strips · 2 shallots, chopped · 1 clove garlic, crushed · 4 tbsp Madeira · 2 tbsp balsamic vinegar · 300 ml (10 fl oz) vegetable broth · 2 tbsp grated parmesan cheese · salt · pepper · paprika · 3 tbsp basic tomato sauce (see p. 9)

Sauté the bacon, shallots and garlic in hot oil. Pour in the Madeira, vinegar and broth and simmer for 20 minutes. Stir in the cheese and spices, then add the tomato sauce. **Good with wild boar steaks.**

Per portion ca. 137 kcal/575 kJ
6 g P · 11 g F · 3 g C

Sherry sauce with chilli

2 tbsp olive oil · 1 finely chopped chilli · 1 clove garlic, crushed · 100 ml (3 fl oz) sherry · 300 ml (10 fl oz) vegetable broth · 2 tbsp olive paste · salt · pepper · cinnamon · nutmeg · 3 tbsp basic brown sauce (see p. 9)

Sauté the chilli and garlic in the hot oil. Add the sherry and broth, simmer for 20 minutes, then stir in the olive paste. Season with spices and thicken with the brown sauce. **Good with goat meat.**

Per portion ca. 125 kcal/526 kJ
1 g P · 9 g F · 3 g C

White bean sauce

2 tbsp olive oil · 3 cloves garlic, crushed · 250 g (9 oz) cooked white beans · 1 tomato, skinned and diced · 300 ml (10 fl oz) vegetable broth · salt · pepper · cayenne · Tabasco Sauce · 3 tbsp basic light sauce (see p. 9)

Sauté the garlic in the heated oil. Add the beans and tomatoes and briefly sauté. Pour in the broth and simmer for 10 minutes. Purée the sauce, season and thicken with the light sauce. **Good with meat fondue and game.**

Per portion ca. 138 kcal/578 kJ
5 g P · 8 g F · 11 g C

Tarragon sauce

2 tbsp sunflower seed oil · 2 shallots, chopped · 1 tomato, peeled and diced · 100 ml (3 fl oz) poultry stock · 4 tbsp vermouth · 100 ml (3 fl oz) white wine · 1 bunch tarragon, chopped · 4 tbsp crème fraîche · curry powder · salt · cayenne · lemon juice

Sauté the shallots in the heated oil, add the tomato and sauté. Pour in the stock, vermouth and wine and add tarragon. Simmer for 20 minutes. Stir in crème fraîche and season with spices and lemon juice. **Good with chicken.**

Per portion ca. 128 kcal/538 kJ
2 g P · 10 g F · 4 g C

Banana sauce

3 bananas · 4 tbsp lemon juice · 4 tbsp curry powder · 2 tbsp sour cream · 3 tbsp ground peanuts · salt · black pepper · cayenne

Crush the bananas with a fork and mix with the lemon juice, curry powder and sour cream. Stir in the peanuts and season to taste with the spices. **Good with grilled meat and meat fondue.**

Per portion ca. 160 kcal/669 kJ
3 g P · 4 g F · 27 g C

Sauces for meat

Poultry cream sauce

Meat of 1/2 grilled chicken · 100 g (3.5 oz)
chopped almonds · 250 ml (9 fl oz) basic light sauce (see
p. 9) · 125 ml (4.5 fl oz) vegetable broth · 100 ml (3 fl oz)
cream · 50 g (2 oz) butter · 1/2 bunch chervil, chopped

Purée the chicken meat and the almonds. Stir the purée
into the light sauce and pour in broth. Heat and allow to
reduce somewhat, then fold in the cream and butter. Stir
in the chervil. **Good with breast of veal and boiled beef.**

Per portion ca. 388 kcal/1628 kJ · 15 g P · 35 g F · 5 g C

Ham and capers sauce

2 chopped onions · 1/2 bunch each parsley,
thyme, chopped · 1 bay leaf · 1 clove garlic · 125 g (4.5 oz)
chopped raw ham · 250 ml (9 fl oz) white wine · 250 ml
(9 fl oz) basic brown sauce (see p. 9) · 50 g (2 oz) butter ·
2 tsp bread crumbs · 4 tsp capers · salt · pepper

Simmer the onions, herbs, garlic and ham in the white
wine for 10 minutes. Add the brown sauce and reduce
somewhat. Toast the bread crumbs in the hot butter, then
mix into the sauce with the capers. Season. **Good with
roast pork and veal.**

Per portion ca. 285 kcal/1197 kJ · 11 g P · 18 g F · 11 g C

Parmesan-sage sauce

1 tbsp butter · 2 tbsp sage leaves, cut into strips · 250 ml (9 fl oz) vegetable broth · 150 g (5 oz) crème fraîche · 2 tbsp basic light sauce (see p. 9) · 80 g (2.75 oz) freshly ground parmesan cheese · salt · pepper

Sauté the sage leaves in the hot butter. Add the broth and crème fraîche and allow to reduce somewhat. Stir in the light sauce and add the cheese while stirring to allow it to melt. Season with salt and pepper. **Good with veal.**

Per portion ca. 234 kcal/983 kJ · 8 g P · 22 g F · 2 g C

Rose hip sauce

1 tbsp butter · 1 finely chopped onion · 5 tbsp rose hip purée · 250 ml (9 fl oz) vegetable broth · 100 ml (3 fl oz) red wine · salt · black pepper · 2 tbsp red wine vinegar · 3 tbsp red butter sauce (see p. 11)

Sauté the onion in the heated butter. Stir in the rose hip purée, then pour in the broth and wine. Simmer for 8 minutes, then season with salt, pepper and vinegar. Finally add the red butter sauce. **Good with veal liver and game.**

Per portion ca. 85 kcal/357 kJ · 1 g P · 2 g F · 11 g C

Sauces for meat

Caper sauce

3 tbsp butter · 1 chopped shallot ·
3 tbsp drained capers (from a jar) ·
350 ml (12 fl) veal stock · 3 tbsp
white wine vinegar · 1 bunch mixed
herbs, chopped · 100 ml (3 fl oz)
cream · 3 tbsp basic light sauce (see
p. 9) · salt · pepper

Sauté the shallots in the butter and
add capers. Pour in the stock and
vinegar and simmer for 20 minutes.
Stir in the herbs and cream. Season
with the light sauce, salt and pepper.
Good with meat dumplings.

Per portion ca. 209 kcal/878 kJ
8 g P · 17 g F · 7 g C

Red cabbage sauce

3 tbsp oil · 2 chopped onions · 100 g
(3.5 oz) cooked pumpkin · 1 peeled and
chopped apple · 1 bay leaf · 2 cloves ·
125 ml (4.5 fl oz) apple juice · 375 ml
(13 fl oz) vegetable broth · 100 g (3.5 oz)
red cabbage (from a jar) · 3 tbsp basic
tomato sauce (see p. 9) · salt

Sauté the onions, pumpkin and apple
in the oil. Add the bay leaf, cloves,
apple juice and broth and simmer
15 minutes. Stir in cabbage, thicken
with the tomato sauce and season.
Good with beef rolls.

Per portion ca. 106 kcal/446 kJ
2 g P · 6 g F · 11 g C

Anchovy and fish sauce

200 g (7 oz) tuna fish (tinned) · 2 tbsp
anchovy paste · 400 ml (14 fl oz) veal
stock · 3 tbsp lemon juice · grated
peel of 1/2 lemon · 2 tbsp capers
(from a jar) · 3 tbsp basic brown
sauce (see p. 9) · salt · pepper

Mix the tuna fish with the anchovy
paste and simmer for 15 minutes in
the veal stock. Add the lemon juice
and peel and stir in the capers. Thick-
en with the brown sauce and season.
Good with smoked pork chop.

Per portion ca. 167 kcal/700 kJ
18 g P · 9 g F · 4 g C

Snail sauce

3 tbsp herb butter · 2 shallots, chopped · 150 g (5 oz) chopped snails in herbs (tinned) · 1/4 bunch mixed herbs, chopped · 300 ml (10 fl oz) vegetable stock · 100 ml (3 fl oz) white wine · 3 tbsp béarnaise sauce (see p. 10) · salt · pepper

Sauté the shallots and snails in the heated butter. Add the herbs, stock and wine and allow to reduce somewhat. Thicken with the béarnaise sauce and season. **Good with veal.**

Per portion ca. 180 kcal/753 kJ
6 g P · 14 g F · 3 g C

Cinnamon-soy sauce

350 ml (12 fl oz) vegetable broth · 4 tbsp each light and dark soy sauce · 1 pinch cardamom · 2 pinches cinnamon · 1 tbsp brown sugar · 1/2 bunch coriander leaf, chopped · 2 crushed garlic cloves · 3 tbsp basic tomato sauce (see p. 9) · salt · pepper

Heat the broth and soy sauces and stir in the spices, sugar and coriander leaf. Simmer for 15 minutes. Add the garlic and thicken with the tomato sauce. Season. **Good with roast pork.**

Per portion ca. 48 kcal/200 kJ
2 g P · 3 g F · 4 g C

Juniper sauce

200 ml (7 fl oz) meat broth · 200 ml (7 fl oz) dark beer · 1/2 tsp caraway seed · 1/2 tsp paprika · 2 tsp garlic powder · 4 crushed juniper berries · 1/2 bunch parsley, chopped · 75 g (2.5 oz) crumbled pumpernickel bread · 3 tbsp basic brown sauce (see p. 9) · salt · pepper

Warm the broth and beer. Stir in the spices and parsley and simmer for 15 minutes. Add the pumpernickel, thicken with the brown sauce and season. **Good with pork strips.**

Per portion ca. 106 kcal/444 kJ
5 g P · 3 g F · 11 g C

Sauces for meat

Kumquat sauce

3 tbsp oil · 2 shallots, chopped · 100 g (3.5 oz) washed and sliced kumquats · 400 ml (14 fl oz) veal stock · 1/2 bunch tarragon, chopped · 3 tbsp béarnaise sauce (see p. 10) · salt · pepper

Sauté the shallots and kumquat slices in hot oil and then pour in veal stock. Simmer for 10 minutes, then stir in tarragon. Thicken with the béarnaise sauce and season to taste with salt and pepper. **Good with venison.**

Per portion ca. 199 kcal/836 kJ · 8 g P · 16 g F · 5 g C

Blackberry sauce

200 g (7 oz) blackberries · 3 tbsp sugar · 3 tbsp lemon juice · 75 ml (2.5 fl oz) dark rum · 325 ml (11 fl oz) water · 3 tbsp basic brown sauce (see p. 9)

Sort, clean and rinse the blackberries. Mix with the sugar and lemon juice. Bring the rum and water to the boil in a saucepan, add the blackberries and simmer for 5 minutes. Purée the sauce to preferred consistency. Thicken with the brown sauce. **Good with roast venison.**

Per portion ca. 114 kcal/479 kJ · 2 g P · 3 g F · 8 g C

Raisin-curry sauce

3 tbsp butter · 3 chopped onions · 2 peeled and chopped apples · 1 sliced banana · 400 ml (14 fl oz) vegetable broth · 100 g (3.5 oz) soaked raisins · 1/2 tbsp curry powder · 100 g (3.5 oz) cream · 3 tbsp basic light sauce (see p. 9) · salt · pepper

Sauté the onions in the butter, add fruit and sauté 2 minutes more. Pour in broth and bring to the boil. Stir in the raisins, curry powder and cream and simmer 10 minutes. Add the light sauce and season. **Good with rabbit ragout.**
Per portion ca. 315 kcal/1323 kJ · 3 g P · 17 g F · 37 g C

White cabbage sauce

2 tbsp butter · 50 g (2 oz) chopped bacon · 1 onion, chopped · 200 g (7 oz) white cabbage cut into strips · 300 ml (10 fl oz) game stock · 100 ml (3 fl oz) white port wine · 1/2 bunch parsley, chopped · 3 tbsp brown basic sauce (see p. 9) · 1/2 tsp each caraway seed, dried thyme and marjoram · salt · pepper

Render the bacon in the hot butter, then add the onions and cabbage and sauté for 3 minutes. Pour in the stock and port and reduce slightly. Stir in the parsley and season with the brown sauce, caraway seed, herbs, salt and pepper. **Good with rabbit ragout.**
Per portion ca. 278 kcal/1166 kJ · 8 g P · 21 g F · 8 g C

Sauces for meat

Dill-mustard sauce

4 chopped anchovy fillets · 4 hard-cooked egg yolks · 1 tsp hot mustard · 2 tbsp fruit vinegar · 125 ml (4.5 fl oz) safflower oil · 1/2 bunch each dill and parsley, chopped · 1 tbsp chopped tarragon · salt · pepper · cayenne

In a bowl combine the anchovy fillets, crushed egg yolks, mustard and half the vinegar. Drizzle the oil into this mixture and beat until creamy with a whisk. Stir in the herbs and season to taste. **Good with cold roast meat.**

Per portion ca. 415 kcal/1743 kJ
14 g P · 40 g F · 2 g C

Broccoli cream sauce

2 tbsp butter · 1 chopped shallot · 200 g (7 oz) cooked broccoli · 250 ml (9 fl oz) veal stock · 100 ml (3 fl oz) cream · 50 ml (2 fl oz) white wine · salt · white pepper · nutmeg · 3 tbsp béchamel sauce (see p. 10) · 1 tbsp finely chopped almonds

Sauté shallots in the butter, then add and briefly warm the broccoli. Pour in stock, cream and wine and simmer 15 minutes. Purée, season and add béchamel sauce. Sprinkle almonds on top. **Good with pork cutlets.**

Per portion ca. 186 kcal/780 kJ
7 g P · 15 g F · 5 g C

Green tomato sauce

4 tbsp olive oil · 2 chopped onions · 2 cloves garlic, chopped · 500 g (17 oz) chopped green tomatoes · 250 g (9 oz) peeled and chopped tomatoes · 125 ml (4.5 fl oz) vegetable stock · 3 tbsp wine vinegar · 2 tbsp sugar · salt · Tabasco Sauce · 1/4 bunch mixed herbs, chopped

Sauté the onions and garlic in the oil. Add the tomatoes. Mix in the stock, vinegar, sugar, salt and Tabasco and simmer 20 minutes. Strain, then stir in herbs. **Good with veal schnitzel.**

Per portion ca. 105 kcal/442 kJ
2 g P · 6 g F · 10 g C

Morel sauce

2 tbsp butter · 1 chopped shallot ·
15 g (1 oz) dried morels, soaked ·
20 ml (scant 1 fl oz) white wine ·
10 ml (.5 fl oz) cognac · 250 ml (9 fl oz)
white butter sauce (see p. 11) · 100 ml
(3 fl oz) crème fraîche · 1 egg yolk

Sauté shallots in the butter. Drain
morels (reserve water) and add to pan.
Pour in the wine and cognac. Sieve
the mushroom water, add it to sauce,
and reduce. Mix crème fraîche and
egg yolk, add to sauce with the butter sauce. Season. **Good with rabbit.**

Per portion ca. 430 kcal/1806 kJ
5 g P · 45 g F · 3 g C

Caribbean fruit sauce

1/2 chopped baby pineapple ·
1 nectarine, peeled, sliced · 50 g
(2 oz) strawberries · 2 tbsp lemon
juice · 400 ml (14 fl oz) blood orange
juice · 1/2 bunch lemon balm,
chopped · 2 tbsp brown sugar · 3 tbsp
basic tomato sauce (see p. 9)

Cook the fruit with the lemon and
blood orange juices for 15 minutes.
Purée, then stir in the lemon balm
and sugar. Add the basic tomato
sauce. **Good with venison cutlets.**

Per portion ca. 94 kcal/395 kJ
1 g P · 1 g F · 21 g C

Chanterelle sauce

3 tbsp butter · 75 g (2.5 oz) chopped
bacon · 2 onions, chopped · 100 g (3.5
oz) chanterelle mushrooms · 200 ml
(7 fl oz) each red wine, game stock ·
1/2 bunch parsley, chopped · 3 tbsp
basic brown sauce (see p. 9) · herb
liqueur · salt · pepper · chilli powder

Sauté the bacon and onions in the
butter. Add the mushrooms and
continue cooking. Pour in the wine
and stock, then stir in parsley. Reduce
somewhat, thicken with the brown
sauce and season. **Good with game.**

Per portion ca. 285 kcal/1197 kJ
5 g P · 23 g F · 6 g C

Sauces for meat

Coconut sauce

3 tbsp oil · 2 chopped onions · 200 g (7 oz) carrots, cut into slivers · 1 dried chilli · 200 g (7 oz) coconut cream · 400 ml (14 fl oz) vegetable broth · juice and peel of 1 lime · 3 tbsp basic light sauce (see p. 9) · salt · pepper

Sauté the onions and carrots in the hot oil, then crumble in the chilli. Stir in the coconut cream, add the broth and simmer for 10 minutes. Blend in the lime peel and juice and thicken with the light sauce. Season. **Good with duck.**

Per portion ca. 142 kcal/595 kJ
1 g P · 12 g F · 7 g C

Rhubarb sauce

500 g (17 oz) rhubarb pieces · 100 g (3.5 oz) sugar · 5 tbsp olive oil · 3 shallots, chopped · 3 cloves garlic, chopped · 1/2 bunch parsley, chopped · 1 tsp each black pepper, ground mustard · 1/2 tsp ground coriander seed · 5 tbsp vinegar · salt

Combine rhubarb and sugar and let draw, then cook for 20 minutes. Heat the oil and sauté shallots and garlic. Stir in the parsley and spices, then mix in the rhubarb. Add vinegar and salt and simmer 10 minutes. **Good with spring chicken or poulet.**

Per portion ca. 265 kcal/1113 kJ
2 g P · 15 g F · 29 g C

Caramel sauce

2 tbsp butter · 2 tbsp sugar · 2 red onions, cut into rings · 200 ml (7 fl oz) beetroot juice · 200 ml (7 fl oz) red wine · 2 tbsp sherry vinegar · 1/2 bunch parsley, chopped · 3 tbsp red butter sauce (see p. 11) · salt · pepper

Caramelise the sugar in the hot butter, then add the onions. Stir in the juice and red wine, add the vinegar and reduce the mixture somewhat. Stir in the parsley. Season with the red butter sauce and spices. **Good with roast chicken.**

Per portion ca. 103 kcal/431 kJ
3 g P · 3 g F · 8 g C

Lemon balm sauce

3 tbsp butter · 2 chopped onions ·
1 clove garlic, crushed · 100 g (3.5 oz)
chopped aubergine · 3 tbsp lime juice ·
350 ml (12 fl) vegetable broth ·
1/2 bunch lemon balm, chopped ·
3 tbsp basic light sauce (see p. 9) ·
salt · pepper

Sauté the onions, garlic and aubergine in the heated butter. Add the
lime juice and the broth. Simmer for
5 minutes. Stir in the lemon balm
and thicken with the light sauce.
Season. **Good with duck.**

Per portion ca. 71 kcal/300 kJ
1 g P · 5 g F · 4 g C

Sea buckthorn sauce

300 ml (10 fl oz) poultry broth · 100 ml
(3 fl oz) white wine · 1 chopped
mango · 4 tbsp Campari · 2 tbsp sea
buckthorn jelly · salt · pepper · curry
powder · 3 tbsp basic tomato sauce
(see p. 9)

Combine the mango, broth and wine
in a saucepan and heat, then stir in
the Campari. Add the sea buckthorn
jelly and spices, then stir in the
tomato sauce. **Good with goose.**

Per portion ca. 131 kcal/548 kJ
5 g P · 6 g F · 10 g C

Honeydew melon sauce

2 tbsp butter · 50 g (2 oz) chopped
pistachios · 200 g (7 oz) chopped
honeydew melon · lemon juice ·
350 ml (12 fl) orange juice · 1/2 bunch
lemon balm, chopped · 2 tbsp sugar ·
3 tbsp basic brown sauce (see p. 9) ·
salt · lemon pepper

Toast the pistachios in the heated
butter, add honeydew melon, lemon
and orange juices and simmer for
15 minutes. Stir in the lemon balm
and sugar, then add the brown sauce.
Season. **Good with duck breast.**

Per portion ca. 151 kcal/633 kJ
3 g P · 12 g F · 8 g C

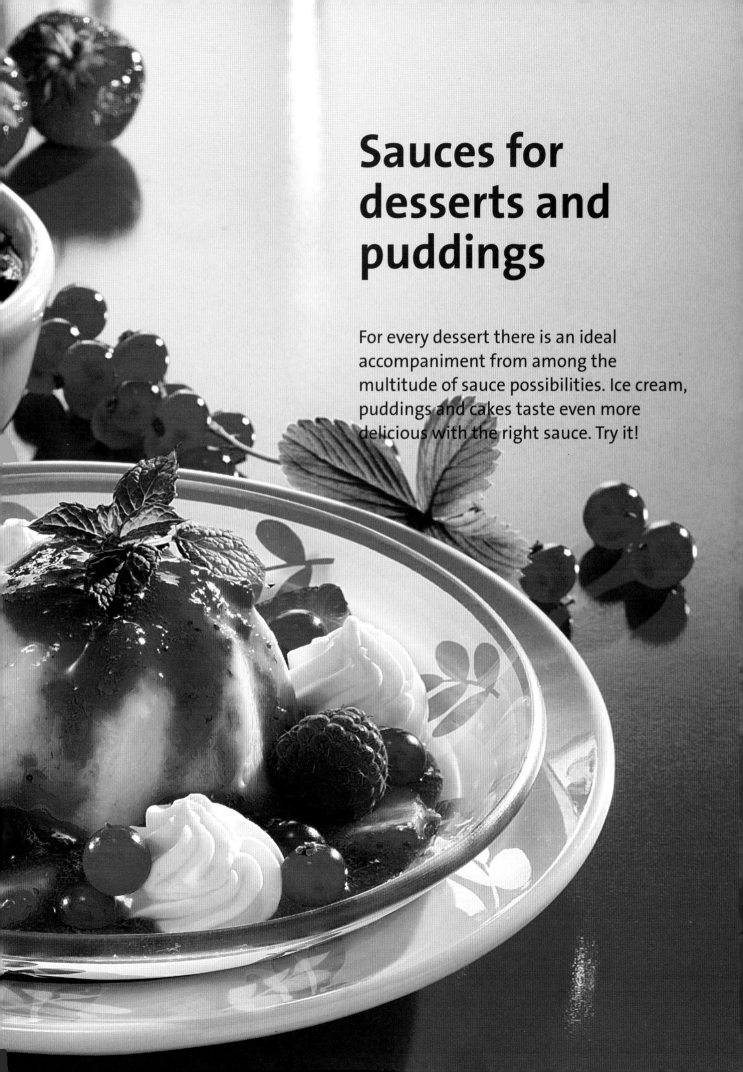

Sauces for desserts and puddings

For every dessert there is an ideal accompaniment from among the multitude of sauce possibilities. Ice cream, puddings and cakes taste even more delicious with the right sauce. Try it!

Dessert sauces

Mascarpone crème

400 g (14 oz) mascarpone

2 egg yolks

50 g (2 oz) icing sugar

1. Turn the mascarpone into a bowl.

2. Add the egg yolks and icing sugar to it and stir everything until smooth.

Good with sautéed apples.

Per portion ca. 425 kcal/1785 kJ
13 g P · 35 g F · 15 g C

Variation 1

Prepare the mascarpone crème as in the basic recipe. Stir in 1 tbsp chopped pistachios and 2 tbsp Marsala. **Good with fresh strawberries and other berries.**

Per portion ca. 388 kcal/1628 kJ

13 g P · 36 g F · 3 g C

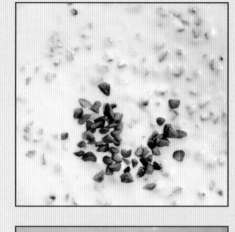

Variation 2

Prepare the mascarpone crème as in the basic recipe. Stir in 1 tsp vanilla essence and 100 g (3.5 oz) cherry or elderberry jelly. **Good with crêpes and pancakes.**

Per portion ca. 508 kcal/2132 kJ
13 g P · 35 g F · 35 g C

Variation 3

Prepare the mascarpone crème as in the basic recipe. Stir in 100 ml (3 fl oz) ready-made chocolate sauce. **Good with ice cream.**

Per portion ca. 443 kcal/1859 kJ
13 g P · 36 g F · 18 g C

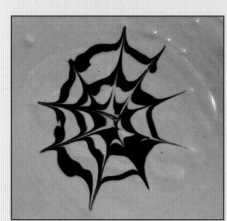

Variation 4

Prepare the mascarpone crème as in the basic recipe. Stir in 30 g (1 oz) dessicated coconut and 50 ml (2 fl oz) pineapple juice. Add Cointreau to taste. **Good with pastries and cakes.**

Per portion ca. 475 kcal/2006 kJ
13 g P · 40 g F · 17 g C

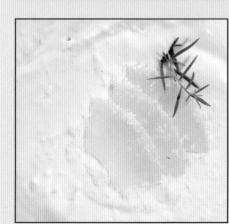

Dessert sauces

Vanilla cream

500 ml (17 fl oz) milk · 1 vanilla pod, split lengthwise · 6 egg yolks · 4 tbsp sugar

Scrape the seeds out of the vanilla pod. Heat them in a
pan with the milk and the vanilla pod. Beat the egg yolks
and sugar in a bowl until foamy and add to the hot milk.
Pour the mixture into the top of a double boiler and beat
for 10 minutes until foamy. When the sauce thickens,
remove the vanilla pod. **Good with apple strudel.**

Per portion ca. 216 kcal/908 kJ · 9 g P · 15 g F · 11 g C

Coffee liqueur sauce

2 tbsp butter · 2 tbsp sugar · 200 g (7 oz) cream ·
2 tbsp coffee liqueur · 2 tbsp sliced almonds

Melt the butter and caramelise the sugar in it. Stir in the
cream and simmer for 2 minutes. Then add the coffee
liqueur and stir well. Toast the almond slices until light
golden brown and stir into the sauce. **Good with puddings
and soufflés.**

Per portion ca. 230 kcal/965 kJ · 2 g P · 21 g F · 7 g C

Orange-wine sauce

Juice of 4 blood oranges · 250 ml (9 fl oz) red wine · 4 tbsp brown sugar · 1/2 cinnamon stick · 3 cloves · 3 allspice berries · peel of 1 orange, sliced into strips · 1 tsp rice flour · 30 g (1 oz) butter

Bring the orange juice, wine and sugar to the boil with the spices and reduce by a third. Remove the spices. Briefly blanch the orange peel in boiling water. Stir the rice flour into some juice, then bind the sauce with it. Stir in orange peel and butter. **Good with ice cream and small tortes.**

Per portion ca. 145 kcal/608 kJ · 1 g P · 12 F · 11 g C

Cognac sauce

400 ml (14 fl oz) cream · 100 g (3.5 oz) brown sugar · seed and mark of 1 vanilla pod · 150 g (5 oz) bittersweet chocolate, chopped into small pieces · 30 g (1 oz) butter · 1 pinch salt · 2 tbsp cognac

Combine the cream, brown sugar and vanilla mark in a saucepan and stir until the sugar dissolves. Simmer for 1 minute. Stir in the chocolate pieces and melt. Finally stir in the butter and salt and add cognac to taste. **Good with pastry and ice cream.**

Per portion ca. 550 kcal/2310 kJ · 6 g P · 39 g F · 45 g C

Dessert sauces

Orange sauce

4 untreated oranges · 3 tbsp white wine · 2 tbsp sugar · 30 g (1 oz) chilled butter · 4 drops almond essence

Cut the peel of 1 orange into strips. Squeeze the juice from all the oranges. Bring the juice to the boil with the wine, orange peel and sugar and reduce somewhat. Stir the butter in shavings into the sauce. Flavour with almond essence. **Good with vanilla ice cream.**

Per portion ca. 154 kcal/645 kJ
2 g P · 7 g F · 19 g C

Mango cream

1 chopped mango · 1 tbsp honey · 1 tbsp lime juice · 40 ml (1.5 fl oz) apricot liqueur

Bring the mango pieces and 100 ml (3 fl oz) water to the boil. Stir in the honey and lime juice and simmer for 5 minutes. Purée and blend in the liqueur. Allow the mixture to cool. **Good with fruit salad.**

Per portion ca. 34 kcal/142 kJ
20 g P · 16 g F · 7 g C

Apricot sauce

350 g (12 oz) apricots · juice of 1 lemon · 375 ml (13 fl oz) dry champagne · 2 tbsp acacia honey

Peel and halve the apricots, then chop the fruit. In a small saucepan combine it with the lemon juice, champagne and honey. Simmer for about 20 minutes. Then purée and cool. **Good with semolina pudding.**

Per portion ca. 131 kcal/551 kJ
1 g P · 11 g F · 16 g C

Wine cream

4 egg yolks · 150 g (5 oz) sugar · mark of 1/2 vanilla pod · 200 ml (7 fl oz) dry white wine · 1 tsp lemon zest

Beat the egg yolks with the sugar and vanilla mark until foamy, then continue to whisk over a double boiler, gradually adding the wine. Stir in the lemon peel. Plunge the pan with the crème in it into ice water and stir until cooled. **Good with puddings and berries.**

Per portion ca. 116 kcal/487 kJ
4 g P · 7 g F · 2 g C

Strawberry sauce

300 g (10 oz) cleaned strawberries · 3 tbsp sugar · 2 tbsp orange juice · 1 tbsp lemon juice · 1/2 tsp crushed coriander seeds · 20 ml (scant 1 fl oz) orange liqueur

Heat the strawberries in a pan with the sugar, orange juice, lemon juice and coriander. Purée the mixture and reheat. Stir in the liqueur and allow to cool slightly. **Good with ice cream and full-cream yoghurt.**

Per portion ca. 58 kcal/242 kJ
1 g P · 1 g F · 10 g C

Chocolate sauce

200 g (7 oz) unsweetened chocolate · 150 ml (5 fl oz) cream · 3 tbsp sugar · 1 tbsp rum

Chop the chocolate into small pieces and melt over a double boiler, stirring constantly. Heat the cream and sugar in a pot and then stir into the chocolate. Stir until very smooth, then flavour with the rum. Serve either hot or cool. **Good with vanilla ice cream, pudding, semolina pudding.**

Per portion ca. 365 kcal/1533 kJ
5 g P · 28 g F · 24 g C

Dessert sauces

Sweet butter sauce

125 g (4.5 oz) butter, softened · 100 g (3.5 oz) sugar · juice and peel of 1 untreated lemon · 1 egg yolk · 8 tbsp cream · 2 tbsp Armagnac

Cream the butter and sugar. Add the lemon juice and peel, stirring constantly. Whisk the egg yolk and cream together, then add to the butter-sugar-lemon mixture. Stir in the Armagnac last. **Good with sweet dumplings and pancakes.**

Per portion ca. 413 kcal/1733 kJ · 2 g P · 34 g F · 26 g C

Passion fruit cream

1 tsp cornflour · juice of 3 oranges · 4 tbsp sugar · 1 tsp grated lime peel · 6 halved passion fruits · 30 g (1 oz) chilled butter in shavings

Stir the cornflour into 2 tbsp orange juice. In a saucepan combine the remaining juice with the sugar and lime peel and reduce somewhat. Add the fruit and seeds of the passion fruits to this sauce with a spoon, bring to the boil, then add the cornflour and thicken the sauce. Stir in the butter shavings. **Good with ice cream, cakes and soufflés.**

Per portion ca. 250 kcal/1049 kJ · 5 g P · 8 g F · 33 g C

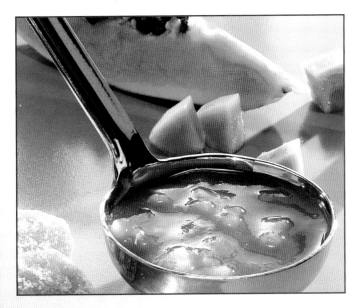

Papaya-ginger sauce

60 g (2 oz) chopped candied ginger · 2 tbsp rum ·
flesh of 2 papayas, cubed · 150 g (5 oz) sugar · 4 tbsp white
wine · mark of 1 vanilla pod

Marinate ginger in the rum for 30 minutes. Set aside
50 g (2 oz) papaya. Mix the rest with the sugar, wine and
vanilla mark. Bring to the boil and simmer 20 minutes.
Purée the fruit and return to the boil. Let sauce thicken
slightly, then add reserved papaya pieces and the rum-
ginger mix. **Good with fruit tortes, ice cream and crêpes.**
Per portion ca. 209 kcal/879 kJ · 1 g P · 12 g F · 49 g C

Fruit sauce

400 g (14 oz) mixed berries (strawberries, blackberries and raspberries) · 150 g (5 oz) sugar · juice of
1 lemon · 8 tbsp cherry liqueur

Clean the berries and rinse. Bring the fruit to the boil with
the sugar and lemon juice in 500 ml (17 fl oz) water and
then let simmer for 20 minutes. Purée the mixture, strain
through a sieve and stir in the liqueur. Serve either hot or
cool. **Good with ice cream, pancakes and yeast pastries.**
Per portion ca. 213 kcal/896 kJ · 1 g P · 1 g F · 46 g C

Dessert sauces

White choco-late sauce

200 g (7 oz) white chocolate · 100 ml (3 fl oz) milk · 200 ml (7 fl oz) cream · 10 ml (.5 fl oz) orange liqueur

Chop the chocolate into small pieces and then melt in the top half of a double boiler. Scald the milk and cream, let simmer for 2 minutes, then stir into the chocolate. Add the liqueur and stir until consistency is perfectly smooth. **Good with ice cream and crêpes.**

Per portion ca. 430 kcal/1806 kJ
7 g P · 32 g F · 50 g C

Rum-egg cream

4 egg yolks · 4 tbsp sugar · 4 tbsp dark rum

Whisk the egg yolks together with the sugar, then place in top half of a boil, beating until the mixture is creamy. Do not allow the water in the bottom half to boil! Combine the rum with 125 ml (4.5 fl oz) water and slowly pour into the cream. Serve immediately. **Good with fruit salads and sorbets.**

Per portion ca. 120 kcal/504 kJ
4 g P · 7 g F · 5 g C

Cherry sauce

500 g (17 oz) sour cherries · 150 g (5 oz) brown sugar · 100 ml (3 fl oz) white wine · 1 tsp custard powder · 2 tbsp kirsch or cherry juice

Wash and stone the cherries. Combine cherries, sugar and wine in 250 ml (9 fl oz) water and bring to the boil. Simmer for about 10 minutes. Purée the mixture to preferred consistency and bind with the custard powder. Flavour with the kirsch or cherry juice. **Good with ice cream and pastries.**

Per portion ca. 255 kcal/1071 kJ
1 g P · 1 g F · 55 g C

Honey sauce

250 ml (9 fl oz) cold full-cream yoghurt · 2 tbsp freshly chopped mint · 3 tbsp sunflower honey

Mix the mint and the yoghurt together in a bowl, blending well. Gradually pour the honey in a thin stream into this mixture and gently fold it in. (The honey may need to be warmed slightly to be sufficiently fluid.) Serve well chilled. **Good with hot pancakes, puddings or fruit.**

Per portion ca. 122 kcal/510 kJ
2 g P · 11 g F · 3 g C

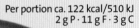

Chestnut sauce

4 egg yolks · 125 g (4.5 oz) sugar · 250 ml (9 fl oz) cream · 4 tbsp chestnut purée · 1 tsp maraschino liqueur · chopped pistachios for garnishing

Combine egg yolks and sugar, then beat in the top of a double boiler over warm water, not boiling, until foamy. Add half of the cream and mix until creamy, then stir in the chestnut purée and cool. Whip the remaining cream and fold into the sauce with the liqueur. Sprinkle with pistachios. **Good with waffles.**

Per portion ca. 410 kcal/1722 kJ
6 g P · 27 g F · 36 g C

Honey-nut sauce

200 ml (7 fl oz) maple syrup · 100 ml (3 fl oz) cream · 1 tbsp cappuccino powder, dissolved in 2 tbsp boiling water · 75 g (2.5 oz) chopped walnuts (or other nuts) · 2 tbsp coffee liqueur

Combine the maple syrup and cream in a saucepan and bring to the boil. Simmer over low heat for 5 minutes or until somewhat thickened. Allow the sauce to cool, then add the cappuccino, nuts and coffee liqueur. **Good with ice cream, pudding.**

Per portion ca. 380 kcal/1596 kJ
4 g P · 19 g F · 44 g C

Index of Recipes